GROWING
A FORTUNE

GROWING
A FORTUNE

---

12 Investment Secrets to Financial Prosperity

STEFAN BECHTEL

SOURCEBOOKS, INC.®
NAPERVILLE, ILLINOIS

This publication is designed to provide accurate and authoritative information in regard to the subject matter covered. It is sold with the understanding that the publisher is not engaged in rendering legal, accounting, or other professional service. If legal advice or other expert assistance is required, the services of a competent professional person should be sought.—*From a Declaration of Principles Jointly Adopted by a Committee of the American Bar Association and a Committee of Publishers and Associations*

This book contains statements that have been obtained from sources believed to be reliable, but are not guaranteed as to accuracy, completeness, or timeliness. The information contained within this book is intended to be helpful as a guideline, and should not be used as a sole research reference when investing. The author and publisher disclaim liability for any losses that may be sustained from investments made resulting from advice espoused in this book.

Published by Sourcebooks, Inc.
P.O. Box 4410, Naperville, Illinois 60567-4410
(630) 961-3900
FAX: (630) 961-2168
www.sourcebooks.com

Library of Congress Cataloging-in-Publication Data

Bechtel, Stefan.
     Growing a fortune: 12 investment secrets to financial prosperity/by Stefan Bechtel.
        p.cm.
        ISBN 1-57071-774-5 (alk. paper)
    1. Investments. 2. Investment analysis. 3. Portfolio management. I. Title

HG4521 .B4242 2002
332.6—dc2

                                                                2001057581

Printed and bound in the United States of America
VA   10   9   8   7   6   5   4   3   2   1

This book is for you.
May your garden always flower
and your fortunes ever flourish.

ACKNOWLEDGMENTS

My great thanks to Peter Dawyot, president of Catawba Capital Management, for reading and commenting on this manuscript (and helping me manage my money)! Ditto to his assistant Melissa Pierce, who spent days poring over my financial records to compute my annualized returns. I'd like to thank Darwin Bayston, certified financial analyst, president of Bayston Capital Management and past president of the Association for Investment Management Research, and his assistant Michael Terry, for contributing ideas and re-crunching my numbers. Thanks to Tom and David Gardner, jingle-hatted founders of the Motley Fool website, whom I've never met but who convinced me that the amateur investor can often beat the pros—and have a ton of fun doing it. I'd also like to thank my sometime coauthor, Laurence R. Stains, for his excellent stylistic and literary comments on my little book. Thanks to my agent, Reid Boates, for taking on the project, and to Hillel Black, executive editor at Sourcebooks, for agreeing to publish it. And finally, thanks to my long-suffering wife, Kay, for putting up with my babbling about the stock market way too early in the morning; and to my kids, Adam and Lilly, for putting up with me at all.

TABLE OF CONTENTS

SPRINGTIME AND PLANTING

SUMMERTIME

AUTUMN AND HARVEST

*I*NTRODUCTION

—

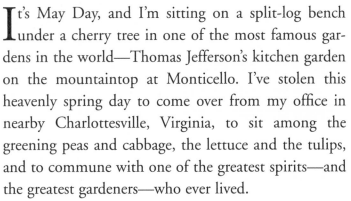

"No occupation is so delightful to me as the culture of the earth, and no culture comparable to that of the garden."

—Thomas Jefferson, letter to Charles Willson Peale

It's May Day, and I'm sitting on a split-log bench under a cherry tree in one of the most famous gardens in the world—Thomas Jefferson's kitchen garden on the mountaintop at Monticello. I've stolen this heavenly spring day to come over from my office in nearby Charlottesville, Virginia, to sit among the greening peas and cabbage, the lettuce and the tulips, and to commune with one of the greatest spirits—and the greatest gardeners—who ever lived.

This two-acre garden was hewn out of the mountainside just below Mr. Jefferson's famous house, and is supported by a massive, thousand-foot-long wall so it seems to hang off of the edge of the mountain like a shelf. On the hillside below this garden, I can see the orchards and vineyards and berry bushes he called his "fruitery," and beyond that, my eye drifts out across the vast plains of the Virginia Piedmont, a vista he called "my ocean," because it looks so much like a great, blue, undulating sea.

On this particular spring day, a clear, blustery afternoon coming after days of cold rain, the kitchen garden is bursting with green and with inventiveness. In Mr. Jefferson's day this garden served as a source of food for the table and also as an amazing horticultural laboratory where he experimented with 250 varieties of more than seventy different species of vegetables. Here he grew beans and salsify collected by the Lewis and Clark expedition, figs from France, peppers from Mexico.

Today, in the restored garden (which closely resembles the original) I find odd varieties of peas—blue Prussians and marrowfats—and immense, crinkly savoy cabbages that look like great green brains in the tender spring sun. There is cauliflower and early blood beets and leeks and comfrey and sage and Jerusalem artichoke. There are wonderful oddities like cardoon, a plant related to artichoke with an edible stem, and hops for beer making, and horehound, and roquette, and red orach. Tucked beside the sun-warmed, south-facing stone wall, sumptuous Marseilles figs are just beginning to unfold their leaves, like little hands.

"The greatest service which can be rendered any country is to add a useful plant to its culture," Jefferson once wrote to a friend. And he tried, mightily, to do so. He was forever exchanging seeds and cuttings with other gardeners in America and abroad, forever shipping things back and forth, forever tinkering with the nature of things. His most ambitious experiment—an attempt to establish the first winemaking industry in

America—was a failure. But, he succeeded in introducing dry rice and olives in South Carolina and Georgia, and sought to identify the one or two hardiest varieties of every single kind of garden vegetable.

His gardens were not only a source of food for the table. His other important crops were food for the soul: beauty, calm, and serenity. He even tried to arrange the vegetable gardens so as to please the eye and satisfy the soul, arranging adjacent rows of purple, white, and green sprouting broccoli. On the great West Lawn of Monticello he created a vast semicircular walkway called "the roundabout," edged on both sides by triple-planted flowerbeds. He called the yearly succession of bloom "my three-act play." The spring bulbs burst first—waves of crocuses and narcissus and tulips. Then came the annuals and biennials—iris, foxglove, Canterbury bells, zinnias, ageratum. And finally, the heat-tolerant midsummer blossoms—poppies, heliotrope, larkspur, and loosestrife.

And…but wait.

I sense you getting restless now. Are you still with me? What's that you say? You thought this was a book about how to make your money grow, and here I am going on and on about how Mr. Jefferson's cabbages look like green brains in the tender spring sun?

Oh, but it *is* a book about how to make your money grow. It *is* a book about successful investing—

hopefully, *very* successful investing. And the *way* I'm talking about Mr. Jefferson's garden—kind of gently lollygaging along, stopping here and there to sniff the bearded iris or savor a sprig of sage—that's about successful investing, too.

Because in this gentle little book, I hope to impart to you a simple, reliable, time-tested plan for dramatically multiplying your money, based on things I've learned in the garden.

I have been a devoted gardener for nearly twenty years now, and a successful investor for almost the same length of time. And puttering among my perennials one day it occurred to me that many of the same principles, attitudes, and habits of mind that I employ in my garden are the very same ones I've employed with such success in the stock market.

I don't believe it's necessary to hang this book on my own personal investing record. This is a sound investing method, which I'll demonstrate with academic studies and the observations of truly accomplished investors. It doesn't matter whether you have twenty thousand or twenty million invested, the principles are the same. (Of course, no investing method works all the time, in every kind of economic climate. But, I hope to convince you that this is a safe, sound method of growing your money in most sorts of economic weather.)

Still, I haven't done too badly. Over the past seven years (December 31, 1994 through December 31, 2001), my stock portfolio returned 35.4 percent per year. That means the total cumulative return over that period of time was 734.6 percent. (These annualized performance numbers were computed by Roanoke, Virginia-based Catawba Capital Management, using an accounting package called Advent, which is widely used by professional investment managers.)

During the first five years of this period, of course, the stock market was topping off the longest-running bull market in U.S. history. My little perennial patch of stocks was absolutely bursting with bloom owing to optimum conditions of sunshine, rainfall, temperature, and soil. (To be perfectly immodest, my annualized returns over that five-year period were 68 percent—a giddy and also unsustainable run.)

But, it was the year 2000 that really required the wisdom, patience, and long-term vision of Jefferson. It was the year 2000 that put the advice in this little book to the test. That year, the NASDAQ plunged almost 40 percent, the worst year since it was created in 1971. This was not a long, slow, steady decline, like a ski trip down the beginner slope. It was a lurching, stomach-churning, up-and-down descent—an almost daily dose of nausea.

The average intra-day volatility of the stocks in the Dow Jones Industrial Average that year was the highest since 1933; the NASDAQ registered the highest volatility since data started being collected in 1985. According to *The Wall Street Journal*, the distance from the NASDAQ's peak to its trough that year represented a drop of 54 percent—an amazing disappearing act in which $3.3 *trillion* dollars of paper wealth simply vaporized.

Wowsa! If anybody needed a calm, Jeffersonian point of view—a gardener's view—that was the time for it. Because Jefferson's whole idea about what a garden is for was—like his ideas about almost everything else—as vast and majestic as the vistas from way up here on his mountain. He wasn't just growing peas; he was trying to change the world. He wasn't just planting for this particular season; he was planting for all time, and for all people. Everything he did, in fact, seems to have been conceived and born out of a vast, calm, long-term view of time and of himself.

It's fascinating to me that, after Jefferson's death in 1826, this garden fell into sad despair and was only resurrected in 1939 by the Garden Club of Virginia. The great "roundabout" arc of flowerbeds, long overgrown with weeds, was rediscovered when perennial bulbs came into bloom in the spring—115 years after the gardener had died!

Jefferson's whole plan for this garden, and for his beloved Monticello, was conceived over such vast expanses of time that it long outlived him. It took him

forty years of tinkering to decide that the house was finally done. He planted and replanted and improved and revised these gardens for most of his lifetime, taking the deepest sort of pleasure from all of it.

We have a great deal to learn about growing a fortune—about building a perennial bed that will long outlive us—from this man.

What's that you say? You think you're wasting your time up here? You can't understand how you can make money sitting underneath a tree? You don't know why this matters?

Well, it matters a lot. It matters because your *attitude* is one of the central secrets of your success or failure in the markets. The great stock-picker Peter Lynch, one of the best ever, has often said that it takes more guts than brains to succeed in the stock market. In other words, the way you behave when things are going badly—like the year 2000—is even more important than your ability to pick the right stocks in the first place. It's your *attitude* that counts.

Sounds simple, doesn't it? Just pick a good stock at a decent price and hang on through thick and thin.

Well, I'm here to tell you that learning patience, calm, and wisdom in the face of gut-wrenching turmoil and volatility in the markets is anything but simple.

"Though an old man, I am but a young gardener," Mr. Jefferson once wrote, alluding to the lifetime of learning it takes to become a truly wise and successful gardener. The same is true of becoming a wise and successful investor.

But, it's not all toil and trouble. In fact, the thing I love most about this method of investing (besides vastly multiplying my money) is that it requires so little effort. It rewards indolence; it celebrates sloth. In many ways, this whole book is an ode to inaction. To get the full effect, it should be read in a hammock on a lazy summer day.

In fact, I want for this whole book to be a garden—a sort of garden of words. A garden that provides both fruit and flower. I want for this word-garden to please your soul, but also to provide food for your table. I want it to be as pleasant to read as a stroll through a shady bower, but as deliciously useful as a bowl of raspberries—a bowl of raspberries that grows bigger and more scrumptious with each passing year.

(I'm going to try to keep the numbers to a minimum in this book. I'd much prefer to talk about your investments in terms of raspberries than in terms of capital gains.)

Obviously, this is a method that stands in sharp contrast to the temper of our times, with all the fevered up-to-the-minute reports from MSNBC, the frantic online trading, the heart-stopping volatility of almost all the indexes, the financial magazines hawking each quarter's "hottest" funds.

Instead, we've come up here to Monticello mountain to spend a bit of time beneath a cherry tree, way up above it all, in a place with a view so grand that you feel you might even be able to see into the next century. We've come here to commune with one of the great spirits and try to learn calmness, patience, and the long, *long*-term view.

I may as well mention here that although Thomas Jefferson's life changed the world, and though he lived very well indeed, he did not build a great personal fortune. In fact, when he died he was worse than broke: he was deeply in debt. Even so, I have no doubt that if he had set his mind to building a fortune he could have done so. Instead, he set his mind to building a world-famous garden, a world-famous house, and—oh, yes—a little thing called democracy.

That's why his house is on the U.S. nickel and his face is on the two-dollar bill.

And that's why we're up here, sitting in this garden. That's why we'll come back up here from time to time in the course of this book, and why we'll also visit other wise old gardeners to see what we can learn about making money grow.

My great hope is that, before we're through, you'll have learned some simple but phenomenally powerful wealth-building tools that will help you grow your money for the rest of your life. If I'm lucky, you'll also carry away some useful new gardening tricks.

And, who knows? Maybe you and I both will have learned a little bit more about how to live a calm, wise, and contented life.

That's worth a fortune in itself.

SPRINGTIME AND PLANTING

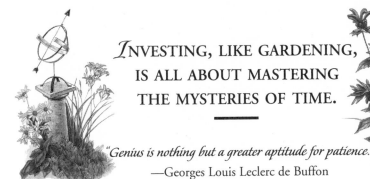

INVESTING, LIKE GARDENING, IS ALL ABOUT MASTERING THE MYSTERIES OF TIME.

"Genius is nothing but a greater aptitude for patience."
—Georges Louis Leclerc de Buffon

There's a certain sly twinkle you often see in the eye of old gardeners. And I'm seeing it now, in the eye of the most masterful gardener I've ever met—Andre Viette, nationally known horticulturist, author, lecturer, and owner of Andre Viette Farm and Nursery in Virginia's bucolic Shenandoah Valley. His 210 acres of fields and greenhouses house one of the most extensive collections of shade- and sun-loving perennials on the East Coast—over three thousand varieties in all. He hybridized many of them himself, like the fabulous Shenandoah cabernet daylily, which has an immense, fleshy bloom the color of a sunset seen through a glass of red wine.

But, besides sitting on all kinds of prestigious horticultural society boards, Andre is also someone who still takes a childlike delight in grabbing a handful of good old garden dirt and taking a big sniff of it. He's kind of a kid, basically. Right now he is sitting at his messy dining room table, and he is smiling at me. He's smiling because I've just asked him how old he is, and he knows he's got me stumped. He has a broad, cheerful Swiss face, enormously powerful hands and forearms, and a voice that booms across the room like a bass drum. His whole presence exudes vitality.

"Well, I prefer not to think in terms of chronological age—but in that sense, I'm sixty-five," he says. "I prefer to think more in terms of biological age, *real* age. In that sense, I'm still a young man. I work every day, seven days a week!"

He sends his wife, Claire, scurrying into the next room to find a book in which the physician-author makes the argument that we can control our "actual" biological age to a much greater extent than most people realize. We can, in effect, learn to master time.

And that's precisely what this chapter is all about.

Learning to become a great gardener means learning to master the mysteries of time. And becoming a great investor also means mastering the mysteries of time.

What sets phenomenally successful investors—people like Paul Allen, Warren Buffet, or Peter Lynch—apart from the vast horde of mediocre, half-bad, or *really* bad investors? One of the primary differences is their calm, long-term, almost Jeffersonian view of time and their place in it. In other words, picking the right stocks is important, but it's not as important as hanging on to them through thick and thin, even when the market bottoms out and your stocks have lost huge chunks of value. The fainthearted fold their cards and walk away from the table. The wise and patient, knowing they've chosen well, just wait. (There are times to hold 'em and times to fold 'em, of course. For more on when and why to sell, see chapter 9.)

This is partly why year after year most investors, as well as most professional money managers, fail to match the S&P 500, a standard benchmark of the overall market's performance. Consider this: according to financial researcher Robert Sheard, who rummaged through the records of 5,845 mutual funds tracked by the Reuters Money Network, over 75 percent of mutual funds fail to match the market average each year. All those highfalutin', highly paid professionals can't seem to beat people who just invest in a market basket of good stocks (or simply buy an index fund, which mimics the S&P 500) and then do absolutely nothing. That's amazing!

In a culture that values speed, convenience, and instant gratification above all else—and that's recently been jolted up to hyper speed by the Internet—most people seem to have turned their backs on the humble, old-fashioned virtues of calmness, patience, and the long-term view.

But not Warren Buffet. The value of his consortium of companies, Berkshire Hathaway, has increased from $18 per share in 1965 to over $60,000 per share in

early 2000, growing his personal net worth to over $31 billion (about equal to the gross national product of Kuwait). Talk about harnessing the power of time! (There's a useful mental trick called The Rule of 72, which helps you figure out how fast your money will grow over time, while at the same helping you think long-term. Just take the annual return from any investment, expressed as a percentage, and divide it into 72. The result is the number of years it will take to double your money. So, with a 20 percent return, your money doubles in around three and a half years, at 10 percent, it takes around seven years.)

And not Andre Viette. In fact, peering out Andre's dining room window, I can see bountiful evidence of his calm, wise, long-term view of things. He moved his family to this quiet farm back in 1976, a quarter-century ago. He was looking for a peaceful, rural setting where he could find open land, good soil, and a place to raise a family and establish a nursery. He'd learned the nursery business at the elbow of his father, Martin, a Swiss immigrant who began growing perennials on Long Island, New York, back in 1929.

"When we moved here there was nothing around this house—no trees, no plants or flowers, nothing," Andre says, gesturing out the window. "But look out there today!" Resplendent in the early summer sun, the grounds around the house are acres of virtual Eden, all open to the public for pleasure and idea gathering. Huge mounds of hostas, dozens of varieties, spill over the borders. There's an especially amazing palette of daylilies, one of Andre's specialties. (Daylilies' Greek name, *hemerocallis*, means "beautiful for a day," but all these varieties, in such great masses, result in months of bloom.) There's also astilbe, Lenten rose, ferns, phlox, yarrow, loosestrife, coreopsis—explosions of color and form.

Now ask yourself: what is the difference between this amazing, world-class garden and most gardens you see?

OK, sure: Andre Viette is a full-time, professional gardener, and he's got tons of help. But, this garden has also been laid out with a grand vision of what a garden *could* be, both in space and in time. The mental stage upon which he set the drama of this garden was vast, spanning decades of growing seasons. His plan was to build a garden so vast and so beautiful that it would outlast his own life.

And that should be *your* plan if you wish to grow a fortune.

Instead, most people plant their garden with only the most narrow-minded and paltry notion of what a garden *could* be. The mental stage upon which they set the drama of their garden is cramped. They generally think no further ahead than the end of the current growing season or bloom cycle—maybe even no further ahead than next weekend, when they want something in bloom for their garden party for show. And the palette of bloom they choose from is entirely predictable: petunias, impatiens, marigolds, mums.

They're as impatient as they are shortsighted. They stick a petunia in the ground and, if it doesn't do well in two weeks, they yank it out and plant another. They plant annuals when they should be planting perennials. They sweat and toil, sticking in and yanking out, when they should be harnessing the monumental power of time and nature, which knows perfectly well what it's doing all by itself. Come the first frost, those impatiens they painstakingly planted in May are gone forever; but, a bed of daylilies or rudbeckia are busily dividing, over and over again, vastly multiplying their efforts. Season after season, they deepen in richness and beauty and variety with only a fraction of additional effort.

Most gardeners' shortsightedness can also be seen in another way: very often people fail to think more than one or two seasons ahead. Plantings become absurdly packed together and eventually the gardener has to yank things out and start over again. In fact, planting things too close together due to a failure to "see through time" is one of the most common mistakes gardeners make, according to the curmudgeonly garden writer Henry Mitchel, author *The Earth Man* and other wonderful books. A few years down the line, they have to go back and yank out a lovely rhododendron or an Alexandrian laurel, which only now is coming into its full glory, but which has grown so large that it's drowning all its neighbors in shade.

By the same token, one of the primary reasons most investors do poorly in the stock market is that they tend to take such a small, narrow, paltry view of time. A veteran money manager told me the story of a client who spent the first ten years of his investing life busily buying and selling shares, frantically jumping in and jumping out of equities every few weeks or months, attempting to "beat the market." (And this was before day trading on the Internet!)

At the end of the decade, he had the courage to look back over his record—and he had one of those life-altering jolts of reality, like knocking back a big slug of rotgut whiskey without ice. He'd have been better off sitting on his hands, having squandered whatever marginal advantage he'd gained on commissions and taxes and mistakes. After ten years, his portfolio was ever-so-slightly above water—but far behind the steady upward climb of the S&P 500.

(To me, the saddest thing about this story is not so much that he failed to grow his money by 10 or 15 or 20 percent a year. It's that all the time he wasted is gone forever. He'd squandered his greatest gift. Think of how many weekends he could have spent fishing, or swimming with his kids!)

A diversified portfolio of blue-chip stocks is like a healthy bed of perennials, just quietly, magically multiplying, even while you sleep. Andre Viette understands all this implicitly.

"People say they're making all this money in the stock market, but I tell them they can't keep up with my daylilies!" he laughs.

If you plant a single healthy daylily bulb in good soil, he explains, by the second season you'll probably have three bulbs. By the third season, those three bulbs will each very likely triple, giving you nine bulbs. The fourth season, you'll have twenty-seven. And, in seven seasons, given good growing conditions, you'll very likely have over two *thousand* bulbs, a veritable cornucopia of color.

You'll probably have to have a daylily dividing party and invite all your friends, just to thin out the beds. (And giving things away, as you probably know, is one of the greatest joys of gardening, as it is of prosperity.)

That's what it means to harness the power of time to grow your garden. That's how Warren Buffet turned $18 bucks into $60,000.

Here are a few key things that the Andre Viettes and the Warren Buffets of the world have learned about mastering the mysteries of time, which you can use to begin growing your own fortune today:

- Time is the most powerful tool you have for building a great fortune or a grand garden.
- It's virtually impossible to grow a great fortune, or a grand garden, without a grand sense of time.
- It takes quite a few growing seasons to develop a dense, healthy, triple-planted perennial bed that's suited to the soil and sun conditions in your garden. And, it generally takes decades to grow your money from a few humble dollars into a life-sustaining stash. We're all in a hurry, but you can't hurry a garden and you can't hurry an investment. They'll grow and change in their own time and in their own way.

This isn't bad news. It's simply a fact. What's so bad about that? Growing a beautiful garden or building a tidy fortune can be one of the most satisfying things you'll ever do.

Hey, what's the rush, anyhow?

Most people don't quite grasp the fact that they've been handed, free of charge, the most awesome wealth-building tool known to man: time. One of the nicest things about this grand gift—the gift of life, actually— is that though nobody knows how much of it you've been given, everybody gets roughly similar amounts. Most people live somewhere between forty and eighty years; nobody lives to be twenty thousand years old, or even two hundred.

In that sense, time is a great equalizer. Though there are people in this world who are thousands or even bazillions of times richer than you are, nobody has been given thousands of times more time. That's one place where you and Bill Gates are actually in the same ballpark. Make use of this great gift!

Consider this: when Albert Einstein was asked to name the greatest mathematical invention of all time, he replied without hesitation, "compound interest."

Compound interest is the exponential growth of money over time if it's left untaxed and undisturbed. In effect, it's the astounding wealth-building power of time (added, of course, to a little bit of money).

To give you a notion why compound interest amazed even Einstein, and why it is the greatest wealth-building tool you have, consider the old story of the Egyptian pharaoh who hired two brothers to build a barn. When the brothers were finished, the pharaoh asked them how they would like to be paid. (The pharaoh, apparently, was unwise enough to trust contractors.) The first brother said, "I would like to be paid with one hundred bushels of corn." So, the Pharaoh agreed. The second brother, with a sly wink, said, "I'd like to be paid with a single ear of corn. But I'd like it to be doubled each day for a month."

The Pharaoh, thinking he had a sucker on the line, agreed. Unfortunately for him, before the month was out the second brother had emptied every single storehouse of corn in the kingdom. (Assuming it's a month with thirty-one days, the actual number of ears would be 1,073,741,824. Yup, that's a *billion*.)

Your untouched investments don't double every day, of course. But they do grow so smartly it's almost beyond belief. The sooner you harness the power of time, the better off you are.

Here is a less Egyptian example. Let's say you planted $1,000 a month into a taxable mutual fund that pays an average 11 percent a year. (That's a reasonable assumption: over the past seventy-two years, stocks have returned an average of 11.2 percent annually, according to Ibbotson Associates.) After ten years on this monthly savings plan, you'd have harvested $216,998 (before taxes). Don't forget, though, that during those 120 months you only tucked away $120,000. The rest—$96,998—was interest. As your principal grew, the interest on it grew, and then the interest itself began to produce interest. That's the miracle of compound interest.

And the miraculous power of compounding grows as the years go by. After fifteen years on your $1,000-a-month plan, your money garden would grow to $454,689. This time, you've contributed $180,000—and you've earned $274,689 in interest. And after twenty-five years, you've got a truly serious harvest: $1,576,133. That's three hundred monthly payments

totaling $300,000, and $1,276,133 in compounded interest.

It's also important to remember that the sooner you put time to work for you, the better off you are. One of the most common mistakes people make is to put off building up a retirement nest egg until mid-life or even later. But, if you encourage your teenage son to start saving before he's shaving, he'll be way ahead of the game.

Consider another example, also featuring two mythical brothers. The first brother begins socking away $2,000 a year at the age of eighteen and does that every year until he's twenty-eight. That means he's tucked away $20,000—and he doesn't save another dime until he retires at the age of sixty-five. Meanwhile, the other brother doesn't begin saving until he's thirty. He tucks away $2,000 each year until he's sixty-five— a total of $70,000. Who retires richer? The brother who started first, and saved less. (This example assumes they both earned the same rate of return.) The first brother simply harnessed the wealth-building power of time, and he did it early.

And—OK, OK: when you start reading books in which the author makes calculations about what would have happened to your money over twenty-five-, thirty-, or even fifty-year periods, it's easy enough to put the book down and walk away. "The *long run* is a misleading guide to current affairs," John Maynard

Keynes once wrote. *"In the long run* we are all dead."
It's hard for most people to think five years ahead,
much less a quarter-century. Yet, there's truly astounding power in cultivating a view that's so calm, and so
long-term that you are looking even beyond your own
lifetime. The Iroquois Indians had a saying: "In our
every deliberation, we should consider the impact of
our decisions on the next seven generations." Now
that's long-term!

I've had my own life-changing encounters with the
moneymaking power of time. In October of 1994, I
took $50,000 from a royalty check and invested in five
carefully chosen individual stocks: Microsoft, Wal-
Mart, Lowe's, First Union Bank, and a little company
called America Online. Veteran stock-pickers like to
refer to something called the Rule of Five: if you pick
five stocks, three generally just lay there, one goes
down, and one goes up. In this particular case, though,
my picks defied the Rule of Five, big time. Lowe's and
Wal-Mart grew only a little, so less than a year later I
sold them both. (Dumb: they've both appreciated
smartly since that time.) First Union Bank doubled,
and then I sold it. Six years later, I'm still holding my
Microsoft shares, which are worth seven times what I
paid for them.

But of the five stocks, AOL was the one that turned
out to be the bean that grew into Jack's beanstalk,

exploding through the clouds and putting out leaves and seeds and flowers so huge that they were almost surreal. I bought two hundred shares for $12,523. At the time, the company had fewer than a million subscribers and was a distant third in the race to build out a national online service (after Prodigy and Compuserve). Its prospects for success, its accounting practices, its hope of reaching profitability, and almost everything else about it were being scorned in the financial press on a regular basis.

It's now nearly six years later, and I just went online to check the value of that investment. After repeated splits, those two hundred shares have multiplied into 21,600 shares worth $1,242,432. (Those numbers would be higher if I hadn't sold off a bit of stock—the only thing about this experience that I regret.) My split-adjusted cost for those original shares, now selling at $58 a pop, was 48 cents apiece. So, I made what Peter Lynch calls a "120-bagger"—120 times my money—in less than six years.

(By coincidence, about the same time I bought my tiny stake in AOL, Microsoft cofounder and multi-billionaire Paul Allen sold his 25 percent stake in the company for about $200 million. Today it would be worth about $14 billion. Sometimes even the great ones need to learn a little more about patience!)

I'm hardly suggesting that every long-term investment will grow like this. In fact, AOL turned out to be one of the best-performing stocks of a high-flying decade. But, the critical thing to remember is that, after making my original purchase, I did, well, nothing. I just sat on my hands and waited. I planted a viable seed in fertile soil, watered it, and watched it grow. Naturally, of course, I kept carefully monitoring the company's story to see if there were any significant changes that might affect the stock price or the company's long-term prospects. I also kept an eye on the Internet message boards, where people reported frantically jumping in, jumping out, and then jumping back in again, thus missing most of the stock's fabulous gains while paying taxes and commissions to boot.

Meanwhile, my little patch of daylilies just quietly kept dividing, season after season.

Over the long haul, a stock's price is generally fairly closely linked to its earnings (profits). The stock's price goes up because the underlying business is growing— its revenues, market share, strategic advantage, but most importantly its earnings. AOL's stock price was growing at a dizzying rate because the company itself— and, eventually, its earnings—were also growing at a dizzying rate. Six years later, AOL is far and away the leading online service, with over twenty million subscribers. Compuserve is now a division of AOL.

Prodigy is a distant, unprofitable also-ran. And, AOL has merged with Time-Warner, thus completing its transformation into one of the world's media mega-monoliths.

Plants also grow over time at a rate that seems nearly miraculous. Where on Earth did that enormous butternut squash actually come from, lying there in the autumn garden like a sleeping animal? It was once a seed the size of my fingernail.

If it came "from the earth," wouldn't it have consumed at least some of the dirt beneath its roots?

To test this reasonable premise, a seventeenth-century Flemish scientist named Van Helmont once conducted an experiment. He planted a willow sapling in a container that held two hundred pounds of soil and gave it nothing but water for five years. At the end of that time, the tree weighed 169 pounds; the soil weighed 199 pounds, 14 ounces. One hundred and sixty-nine pounds of tree flesh had sprung from two ounces of soil.

The power of photosynthesis to run the engines of plant growth, and the power of time to increase the value of a well-chosen stock portfolio, are equally awesome.

It's no wonder there's such a friendly and natural connection between people who have built great fortunes and great gardens. The Duponts, the Rockefellers, the Carnegies—they were all devotees and masters of the "time garden."

One of my personal favorite time gardens is the Morton Arboretum in Lisle, Illinois, created by Joy Morton, who was the founder of the Morton Salt Company. In December of 1922, when he was sixty-five years old, he laid out a grand plan and began transforming his estate in suburban Chicago into an arboretum that would last long after he was gone and would give pleasure to thousands.

"I want something to develop during the balance of my life on ground for which I have a personal affection, and I hope the work may prolong my life," he wrote his son.

On 735 acres, he laid out plans for ponds, lakes, and roads. There would be groves of maples and spruce and buckeyes, azaleas and rhododendrons, honeysuckle and viburnum. A woodland glade would be filled with tens of thousands of daffodils. There would be a small prairie, planted with native grasses and a grove of trees native to central and western North America, one from the Appalachians, another from northeast Asia.

Grainy old photographs from those early days show men planting trees in what look like empty cornfields. At that time, no doubt, Morton's estate was far from the encroaching city. Today, though, eighty years later, the Morton Arboretum is an oasis of green in a world that has been kidnapped by cars. The open fields that surrounded the arboretum are now subdivisions and strip malls. Joy Morton may not have been able to envision that, but he knew how to envision a garden.

He had such a long view that both his company and his garden outlived him, like the nineteenth-century Scottish lords who brought home redwood seeds from California but never lived to see them towering over their manor houses like craggy, transplanted titans.

But what could be more wonderful, or more worthwhile, than to be outlived by a beautiful tree, a beautiful garden, or a beautiful fortune?

The critical task of an investor, a gardener, or anyone, for that matter, is to "get on the right side of time."

In so many dreary ways, we're all on the wrong side of time, most of the time. There never seems to be enough. You're always running out of it. No matter what you do, you just keep getting older. How do you get on "the right side" of the inexorable flow of time, so that the more time that passes, the better off you are? Well, you can't stop growing older. (Despite great effort, I've never succeeded, anyhow.) But, you *can* sock your money away in a smart, diversified portfolio and let it grow all by itself, so that as you grow older you're also growing richer. (That doesn't solve all your problems, but it helps.)

It's just the same as harnessing the power of time to multiply your daylilies so that each passing season only magnifies the glory of your garden.

Getting on "the right side of time" by having a calm, long-term view of your investments also enables you to overcome many shortcomings, allowing a person of ordinary intelligence to compete with the greatest geniuses. Maybe you can't pick a stock that triples in a year, but if you have the patience to wait, eventually you'll almost certainly be rewarded by tripling, quadrupling, or mega-pling your money.

A wise, dead Frenchman, George Louis Leclerc de Buffon, put it this way: "Genius is nothing but a greater aptitude for patience."

And, by the way, simply putting your money to work in a smart way is not really all that's required to be "on the right side of time." Because now, early in the twenty-first century, we have this odd development: people are making fortunes in the stock market, yet in terms of time they are completely poverty stricken. The richest people in our culture are the most time-poor.

The Washington Post reported that high-flying Wall Street stock analyst Henry Blodgett, who reportedly makes over $4 million a year and can move the market with a single quote, says he and his team of seven associate analysts write three or four reports a week on

about thirty-five companies. "We're absolutely running flat out," he told the *Post*. "At this pace, in another year or two I'll drop dead."

He has no time to return phone calls or email. He cleaned out his "in" basket a few days ago but already he has 720 unread messages. He doesn't even have time to decorate his office, which he's been in for almost a year. His possessions are in boxes on the floor or shoved under the desk. He leaves the office at 8:20 P.M., goes home and works in bed (since there's no couch in the apartment yet and the desk is cluttered with boxes, there's no place else to work). By 6 A.M the next morning he's back in the office.

"This life is totally grueling, totally unsustainable," he said.

But what does this mean? How is it that paper billionaires can be so time-poor?

This is nuts—a peculiarly twenty-first century kind of nuts.

The point of managing your money properly is not only to harness the power of time, but to have time left over to do with it as you wish. If it's been put together correctly in the first place, a good portfolio, like a good perennial bed, can go on blooming for years with almost no attention at all. Its primary "dividend" is not money; it's lazy summer weekends spent doing whatever you please.

As a practical matter, the longer your time horizon, the lower your risk. There's something else about a long time horizon that works to your favor, and puts you on the right side of time: it lowers your risk.

One of the great, unchangeable realities of the market is that the short-term performance of any stock is impossible to predict. But, the longer your time horizon, the lower your risk. According to information provided by the research firm Ibbotson Associates, if you examine every five-year interval from 1926 through 1998 (in other words, 1986–90; 1987–91; 1988–1992, etc.) you find that stocks beat corporate and Treasury bonds, T-bills, and inflation fifty-eight times out of the sixty-nine periods. But, if you stretch your time horizon out to fifteen-year periods, stocks were the best asset fifty-five times out of fifty-nine. And, over twenty-year intervals, stocks had a perfect score: fifty-four out of fifty-four.

The notion that time reduces the risk of holding stocks has sometimes been challenged by academic studies. So, Jeremy Siegel, a finance professor at the Wharton School of the University of Pennsylvania, took a look at almost two centuries of financial data to see if this idea was actually true. "Although stocks are certainly riskier than bonds in the short run, over the long run the returns on stocks are so stable that stocks are actually *safer* than either government bonds or

Treasury bills," he reported in his 1994 book *Stocks for the Long Run.* "The constancy of the long-term, after-inflation returns on stocks was truly astounding." Consider the "time cost" of your investments.

One of the many mysteries of time is that it is a powerful, inexorable force, yet it's also as ephemeral and delicate as a butterfly's wing. Once it's gone, it's gone forever—poof, vanished. There is no "rewind" button on the years spent pursuing the wrong career path. You can't get back the months or years you spent in a bad relationship. Money is not usually like that: the account balance in your IRA may drop, but eventually it will probably come back.

A lost weekend, by contrast, is gone forever.

That's why it's critical to consider the "time cost" of all your investments as well as their financial cost. If time is the most valuable asset that you have, then the loss of time can be considered a cost of owning something. Money managers talk about the "opportunity cost" of investments—that is, the opportunities you might miss by tying your money up in, say, a piece of raw land or a municipal bond. Well, upkeep—"time cost"—is something else you should remember before buying something. A boat, especially a wooden boat, is an asset that brings with it enormous time costs. (Of course, if you enjoy working on boats it's not a liability at all. But if you *don't*, you'll probably wind up losing more than you gain.)

By contrast, one little-recognized aspect of owning common stocks is the fact that owning them takes so little time. Its "time cost" is amazingly low. Compared to lots of other things you could own (like rental real estate, say) stocks take almost no time at all. Beyond regularly perusing the financial pages (and ignoring most of what you read), you can manage a small portfolio in a few hours a week, or less. And, you can do that any time you like. You're not under the gun to go fix somebody's potty, mow the grass, or collect rent checks. There's never anybody breathing down your neck, forcing you to do something immediately.

The time you've saved can be spent—where else?— in the garden.

SPEND A LONG, LONG TIME PREPARING THE SOIL AND SELECTING A VIABLE SEED.

"And the Lord God planted a garden eastward in Eden; and there he put the man whom he had formed...And the Lord God took the man, and put him into the garden of Eden to dress it and keep it."
—Genesis 2:8,15

If somebody had $100 to spend on a garden, I would probably tell them to spend $60 to $70 in good soil preparation and the rest in plants," says Andre Viette, the jolly king of gardeners and one of the biggest growers of perennials on the East Coast. "I would much rather a person buy less plants from me and put them in soil that looks like chocolate pudding. When plants go into soil like that they'll say, 'Yeah, oh boy, I love this!'"

Good soil, Andre says, "smells fresh and alive." With the right soil, you can practically get an axe handle to grow leaves. He chuckles and rubs his hands together, thinking about the beauty and power of that kind of soil.

Andre's advice is a great way to help your vegetables and flowers thrive—and it's a great way to make your portfolio grow. Because as a general thing, you should spend vastly more time "preparing the soil" and "selecting a viable seed"—studying and then selecting your investments—than in tending to them. Andre's percentages sound about right: 60 to 70 percent of the time you spend on your investments, perhaps even more, should be spent doing the research necessary to pick good investments in the first place. After that, you don't need to do much except weed and water. (That is, just follow their progress in the papers and make sure their story has not changed.)

Nothing will ever grow without properly preparing the soil, and it's unlikely that you'll ever make a spectacular investment without thoroughly researching it first. Take it easy. Take your time. What's the rush? As a Wall Street wag once remarked, "buy in haste, repent at leisure." Consider this a pleasant, contemplative task—in fact, one of the most pleasurable and productive tasks a gardener-investor has to perform.

After all, don't you take enormous pleasure in turning up the soil in spring before a single seed gets laid down in the dark?

I'll sometimes spend a few dreamy days out in the garden with hoe, shovel, rototiller, and whatever soil amendments I plan to add that year. I'll mix up my own special confection of "superdirt" in my garden cart, turning in spadefuls of brown-black compost and decomposed leaf loam and a little sand and a little woods dirt for good measure. It's irresistible to just turn that soil over and over in the cart, admiring it, smelling it, thinking how happy your seeds will be to find themselves coming alive in it.

We think we're so important, but if it weren't for ten inches of topsoil and the fact that it rains, we wouldn't be here at all.

The spring chore of preparing the soil is especially important here in Virginia, where the scenery is beautiful but the soil is poor.

We tend to have very little topsoil and a heavy hardpan of heavy red clay—brick-making material. The stuff is so hard that in colonial times, buildings were erected directly on the soil without any foundation at all. All soils contain three different sizes of particles—sand, the largest; silt, mid-sized; and clay, the smallest. The proportion of each determines the soil's water-holding capacity, with sand holding the most and clay the least. So, the task of the Virginia gardener is to overcome the heavy soddenness of our native clay, which also inhibits the exchange of atmospheric gases (mainly carbon dioxide and oxygen), which are so important to a plant's health.

"The biggest mistake many young people make is they'll buy anything they see in bloom and then they'll ask me what grows in red clay," says Andre. "I tell them, 'Nothing grows in red clay.' You're not supposed to plant in red clay; you're supposed to fix the red clay."

In the same way that fixing the red clay is absolutely critical to growing healthy plants, good research is absolutely critical to the success of your investments.

But picking stocks does not have to be a daunting, miserable task, like digging a ditch in red clay. Look, it ain't rocket science. You don't have to *run* a company; you just have to buy a few of its shares and hold them for the long-term.

In fact, the brokerage houses and professional investment services really enjoy making it all sound more complicated than it needs to be. In a famous essay examining the reasons why professional money managers often do so poorly, financier David L. Babson observed that part of the reason is that "they try to make investing into a very complicated job when it is quite a simple and common sense process if you have the discipline to follow a consistent, long-range invest-ment philosophy. You don't have to have a degree from the Harvard Business School to know that Eastman Kodak is a unique company...Nor do you have to be able to spiel a lot of jargon about 'Beta' to know that investors who have bought Minnesota Mining and similar leading stocks over the years have had excellent results without taking much risk or even trying very hard."

Warren Buffet said it even better, "Techniques shrouded in mystery clearly have value to the purveyor of investment advice," he wrote. "After all, what witch doctor ever achieved fame and fortune by simply advis-ing, 'Take two aspirin?'"

One thing to remember: you're never going to get it exactly right. Too much lime, too little; too much sand, too much clay. A clematis planted against a stone wall will simply refuse to thrive, no matter what you try. In the same way, you're never going to be completely successful in your stock picks: nobody is.

John Doerr is a widely admired "starmaker" of Silicon Valley, who has put money behind dozens of high-tech companies and sits on the board of Netscape, Amazon.com, and Sun Microsystems. His investing record is stellar. Yet, he told *The Washington Post* in an interview: "I was dead wrong" about having missed UUNet WorldCom, which he thought couldn't possibly make money by simply renting phone lines from other companies. "I'd be embarrassed to tell you the number of times I've been really wrong," he said.

If John Doerr makes plenty of mistakes, don't worry about your own—or expect not to make them.

Just be sure you do your best to work the soil, and pick a seed that will grow.

TEN WAYS TO TELL IF A SEED IS VIABLE... OR A STOCK IS WORTH BUYING

A seed is an amazing thing, perhaps one of nature's most amazing creations. It's a packet of DNA the size of a thumbnail. But, how do you tell the difference between a live seed and a dead one? What forces are awakened when it makes contact with water, sun, and soil? And, how do you tell the difference between a seed that will grow robustly over many years, and one that's likely be a sickly grower or fizzle out completely after a few seasons?

How you structure your investments is dictated by many personal variables, of course: how much you have to invest, how old you are, your tolerance for risk, your time horizon. But, on the equity side of your portfolio, I'd like to make a case for considering building a smallish, diversified portfolio of individual stocks, rather than (or in addition to) mutual funds.

For one thing, Princeton finance professor Burton Malkiel points to one study that shows if you choose twenty well-diversified individual stocks, it reduces your risk by up to 70 percent. Adding still more stocks to your portfolio does not significantly reduce your risk exposure. In fact, I'd argue that it's difficult to keep track of even twenty stocks. One time-tested rule of the National Association of Investors Corporation, which represents thousands of amateur stock-picking clubs, is to hold no more stocks than you're able to stay informed about. If you can keep on top of 20 stocks, that's impressive. Most people can't do it.

By holding individual stocks, you put yourself ahead of the game in several ways. You avoid fund management fees, which can be surprisingly high, shaving off part of your gains and putting it in the manager's pocket instead of your own. Individual stocks allow you to have much more control over your personal tax situation, since you don't pay any capital gains taxes until you sell your shares. Mutual funds, which may buy and sell hundreds or thousands of issues during the year, generate a tax bill you can't control. And, though mutual funds do provide a certain stability because they invest in so many equities, they also virtually guarantee mediocre returns.

There's something else about holding individual stocks that a gardener would understand. When you invest in a stock you are buying a part of a company—a real thing, which generally has bricks, mortar, management expertise, a product, revenues, inventory, and all the rest. But, when you buy a mutual fund that holds shares in an ever-changing roster of hundreds or thousands of companies, it turns into a numbers game.

"How'd you do?"

"I'm up 25 percent."

"What are you invested in?"

"Beats the heck out of me."

Holding individual stocks gives you some contact with a real company. It's like bringing yourself back down to the ground by plunging your hands into the dirt. Which, after all, is where we came from and where we'll go.

What follows are ten suggestions for identifying stocks that have a good chance of robust growth, no matter what the weather.

Plant things that you know and like.

In the garden, you'd never think of planting perennials that you don't find innately attractive or vegetables whose taste you don't care for. Why would you plant rutabagas if you can't stand them, or goldenrod if you had hay fever?

By the same token, you shouldn't buy anything for your portfolio that you don't instinctively understand, appreciate, or actually use. You stand a much better chance of picking a viable seed if you stick with a small assortment of plants and flowers with which you're familiar. Though it's often said that you shouldn't "fall in love with a stock," there's nothing wrong with having a bit of affection for it, because affection means that you know it and like and use it. That means other people probably do, too.

Fidelity's Peter Lynch is perhaps the greatest apostle of the notion that you can do very well as an amateur stock-picker, often even better than the professionals can, by sticking to stocks about which you have some common sense knowledge. As proof, he points to a seventh-grade class at St. Agnes School in Arlington, Massachusetts, who in the early 1990s produced a 70 percent gain over two years on an imaginary stock portfolio of fourteen companies. During the same period, the S&P 500 was up only 26 percent. How'd the kids do it? They picked stocks they liked and understood, or whose products they used—L.A. Gear, Disney, Gap, Limited, Wal-Mart.

Lynch is sometimes criticized for making stock-picking seem so simple that even a seventh grader can beat the experts. And, it's true that seventh graders can also do as badly as the experts can. But, the basic point is sound: you and everybody else have a certain body of specialized knowledge that can be used to increase your chances of success in the marketplace. Exploit that common sense knowledge; it's part of your competitive edge. If you work in accounting and there's a new piece of software that all the accountants are using, start thinking about its manufacturer as a potential investment. If there's a new toy your kids and all their friends are dying for, take a look at the company, its competitors, and its potential for growth. If a new franchise opens up in your neighborhood and always seems to be mobbed, think of it as a potential investment opportunity.

Who's number one?

A summer meadow may look like a beautiful carpet of grasses and bloom, but actually it's deadly warfare. Plants are engaged in a bitter struggle for dominance, for their fair share of limited resources. They fight all other plants for sunlight, water, atmospheric gases, and soil nutrients, and they'll use every trick in the book to get what they need to survive. Some plants even use a really dirty trick called *allelopathy* (literally, "mutual suffering") in which growth-inhibiting chemicals are spewed into the soil around the plant, a sort of "scorched earth" approach to botanical defense. (Ever notice how almost nothing grows underneath a walnut tree?). If this sounds suspiciously like the world of business, you're absolutely right. Business is also a life-or-death struggle, and many—probably most—businesses lose the struggle. The process is especially unforgiving in the world of the "new economy," where Internet dot-coms and hot-coms can become dot-bombs almost overnight.

When you're looking for a robust, strong-growing stock, one that's likely to keep muscling its way into the sunlight no matter how stiff the competition, it's good to ask yourself, *"Who's the number one player in an industry or a trend that seems destined to survive?"*

First, you pick a trend that you believe has the potential for enormous growth—say, wireless Internet access. Then you look for the leader or leaders in that field—in this case, the six hundred–pound gorilla being the Finnish cellular telephone giant Nokia. The company has strong financials and a dominant position in the cellular telephone market, which many analysts predict will morph into handheld devices that allow you to log onto the Internet as well as chat with aunt Sally.

It's easy enough to determine which company currently has the biggest market share in its industry, a key indicator of dominance. Such numbers can be found in financial newsletters such as the *Value Line Investment Survey* (available free in most public libraries) or on financial sites on the Internet like Bloomberg (www.bloomberg.com) or Hoover's Online (www.hoovers.com). It's a bit more difficult to answer the question, *Can this company maintain its dominance over the next three to five years?* If the company's biggest money-maker is a drug whose patent is about to expire, or a product that could easily be "knocked off" more cheaply by a leaner, meaner company, its dominance could be short-lived. But, if your research leads you to believe that it can maintain its strategic advantage over the foreseeable future—and three to five years into the future is about as far as *anybody* can see—you may have a good bet.

Going with the dominant leader in a promising field is the general method recommended by Mary Meeker, a stock analyst at Morgan Stanley Dean Witter who's become something of a celebrity for her ability to spot winners in the tech world.

"Remember Microsoft versus Lotus; Cisco versus Wellfleet; Dell and Compaq versus Everex," she's written.

You've never heard of Everex? Well, that's just the point.

Even though Meeker has been one of the Internet's biggest cheerleaders, she also warns that many, if not most, Internet companies will fail. That's why going with the leaders gives you a much greater margin of safety in a business world that's as fiercely competitive as your tomato patch.

Is it a good story?

Taken by itself, the idea of buying "story" stocks can turn into a speculative game. But, combined with a sober assessment of a company's financial prospects, it's really not a bad idea at all to look for stocks that have a compelling story to tell. After all, we live and die by stories. Politics and lawyering are all about story-telling; most religions are based on stories (the Bible is called "the greatest story ever told"); "consumer confidence" in the economy is really just belief in a story; and, of course, our favorite story of all is the story of our own lives.

Burton Malkiel, author of *A Random Walk Down Wall Street*, points out that stocks are bought and sold by humans, who are not mathematical machines but emotional beings. Stocks with stories that produce a warm, fuzzy feeling in investors can sell at high multiples for an amazingly long time, even if their fundamentals are weak. By contrast, stocks with sound fundamentals but a lame or boring story are often very slow to catch fire.

"Ask yourself whether the story about your stock is one that is likely to catch the fancy of the crowd," he advises. "Is it a story from which contagious dreams can be generated? Is it a story on which investors can build castles in the air—but castles in the air that really rest on a firm foundation?"

The story should be compelling but simple. Peter Lynch likes to say you should be able to tell this story in ninety seconds or less. "It's a chain of '50s drive-ins where the waitresses are on skates." "It's a disc drive that stores fifty times as much memory as the old kind." "It's a cure for the common cold." (Well, scratch that one.) Just remember that for a stock to catch on, this story has to be told thousands of times, to thousands of different people—entrepreneurs tell it to venture capitalists and banks and fund managers; banks tell it to their boards of directors; stockbrokers tell it to their clients, and so on. If everybody likes the story, you may well have a winner.

Try to catch it early.

While there's still negative publicity and the outcome seems uncertain try to catch it. This, of course, is the point in the process where the risks—and the potential rewards—are greatest.

Paul Hawken, author of *Growing a Business* and cofounder of the Smith and Hawken catalogue company, says that if you have an idea for a business and everybody you talk to says, "Hey, that's a great idea!" it's too late. You've missed the wave. Somebody else is already doing it. The same is true of stocks that haven't quite caught on yet: if everybody knew and loved them, the period of most dramatic appreciation would already be over and the price would be too high.

When I first started buying America Online in late 1994, the fledgling company was beset by bad publicity. The mainstream financial press seemed to go out of their way to lambaste the company. There were questions about AOL's accounting practices, its marketing practices, its lack of earnings, even its business model. Lots of smart people said it was never going to work. Meanwhile, it was a distant third in the race to build out a national online service, behind rivals Prodigy and Compuserve.

But I'd tried Prodigy, and found it juvenile and cluttered with ads. I tried Compuserve and found it pedantic and clumsy and difficult to use. America Online, by contrast, was a cinch to use. It was the Internet on training wheels. Besides its simplicity, I liked the way it was organized, its depth of content, its array of services. And, I was dazzled by being able to instantly check the balance of my stock portfolio, rather than peering into the newspaper stock pages and checking them individually the next day.

My experience convinced me that AOL was going to be a hit, especially among "newbies" to the Internet—of whom tens or even hundreds of millions were waiting in the wings. I really didn't care what *Barron's* thought about it. Now, of course, the United States and most of North America is a minor subsidiary of America Online. But because the company has grown so big, and is so widely known and widely traded, most of the almost unbelievable growth of those early days is over. I made over one hundred times my money in six years, but I could never do it again (at least not on AOL).

Do it regularly.

Gardener-investors who wish to bring a patient, long-term view to the turbulence of the markets can learn to do so by meditating in their Zen garden. Or, they can employ an old, time-tested trick called "dollar-cost averaging." This fancy-schmantzy-sounding technique might also be called the Trying Very Hard Not to Behave Like an Idiot method of making money in the market. In effect, it's a form of self-discipline that helps you keep from becoming a euphoric idiot when the market starts spiraling up into the stratosphere, or a panicked idiot when it starts spiraling down towards the center of the Earth.

The basic idea is simple—in fact, Warren Buffet's hero, Benjamin Graham, described it as ultrasimple in his classic book on value investing called *The Intelligent Investor*. Dollar-cost averaging simply means investing equal dollar amounts in an individual stock or fund, on a regular basis, over a long period of time. By not investing all your money, all at one time, you help to smooth out the peaks and valleys of a market that is guaranteed to have its ups and downs. It's a way of removing your (notably unreliable) emotions from the whole process of stock-picking. It's like calmly planting a crop each season, year in and year out, no matter what the weather is doing.

Sure, it's ultrasimple, but so what? It works, and it's been shown to work for a long, long time. In his great, gray book, Benjamin Graham describes a great, gray study of dollar-cost averaging. This study took a look at twenty-three ten-year periods, beginning in 1929 and ending in 1952, in which a hypothetical investor invested the same dollar amount, once a year, in a representative marketbasket of stocks in the Dow Jones Industrial Average. The average profit at the end of each buying period, not including dividends, was 21.5 percent. Naturally, there were down years in each period, but by the end of the ten years the hypothetical investor was richer and presumably happier than he was at the beginning. The author of this study concluded that "no one has yet discovered any other formula for investing that can be used with so much confidence of ultimate success, regardless of what happens to security prices, as dollar-cost averaging."

Here's how it works. Let's say you decide to invest $2,500, twice a year, in Psychic Crimesolvers Incorporated, figuring that *that's* one heck of a story stock. You mark it in your gardening calendar: every May 15th, when you're planting your garden, you'll spend $2,500 to buy however many shares you can get at the current price. You'll do the same every November 15th, when you're putting the garden down for the winter.

The first time you buy, Psychic Crimesolvers is trading at $20, so your $2,500 gets you 125 shares. Next time, it's slipped to $18, so your $2,500 gets you 138 shares. Then the crime rate drops, and so does the stock price—down to $10 per share. So, you pick up 250 shares. Then the company announces it has solved the O.J. Simpson case—*and it wasn't O.J.!*—and its stock soars to $40 a share. This time, your money only buys 62 shares. But, here's the beauty part. At the end of the day, with four equal purchases spread out over two years, you've spent $10,000 to accumulate 575 shares, at an average cost of $17 per share. Is your investment still worth the $10,000 you put into it? No. The value of those shares has appreciated to $23,000.

By having the discipline to keep buying the same dollar amount of shares, it forces you to buy more shares when they're cheap and fewer when they're expensive. It doesn't matter what the market is doing.

In fact, paradoxically, a prolonged downturn in the price of Psychic Crimesolvers, or the market in general, is exactly what you want, because when the stock's price eventually recovers, the average price of your shares will be far below the market. The main risk, of course, as Andrew Tobias points out in *The Only Investment Guide You'll Ever Need*, is that the stock price goes down and stays down, or the company goes out of business completely. It happens. Which is why you need to try very hard to pick sound stocks in the first place.

Is the company run by good people?

A company's earnings per share, its debt burden, its strategic advantage over its competitors—all that stuff matters. But, so does the character and competence of the people in charge. Whether they're honest. Whether they're candid. Whether they tend to waffle when things go badly. Whether they have vision—and the ability to create that vision.

Tom and David Gardener, creators of the popular Motley Fool website, have observed that it's people who are the "DNA of your company." In biology, they point out, "DNA codes for proteins, and it is the proteins that express an organism's traits. The DNA, debatably, is the single greatest influence on an organism's future. So, too, in the realm of business. People, as a company's DNA, code for actions. Those actions lead to consequences that will ultimately determine your company's (and your investment's) fate. People are the single greatest influence on a company's future."

When assessing a potential investment, Warren Buffet also puts great store in the people who run the company. He wants to know if they make rational decisions, if they know how to allocate limited resources, and especially if they're candid about what's really happening in the company. He admires managers who can admit failure openly, because all managers make mistakes but most can't or won't admit it.

In fact, in the Berkshire Hathaway annual report, Buffet has instituted a wry section called "Mistake Du Jour," a kind of personal wailing in which he plainly lays out whatever error or lost opportunity he feels he committed the previous year. This is important, he says, because "the CEO who misleads others in public may eventually mislead himself in private." He also provides his shareholders with far more information than is required under generally accepted accounting practices, reporting separately the earnings of each of Berkshire's businesses and anything else an investor might need to understand what's actually going on. (Critics say, sure Buffett is candid—that's because he owns over 40 percent of the common stock and can't be fired. Nevertheless, his point is well taken: if you don't trust the company to be straight with you, don't invest in it.)

Nowadays it's easy enough to find out all kinds of things about a company's top brass by using the Internet. One tremendously powerful search engine is Google (www.google.com), which scans over a billion web pages in a few seconds. (Don't ask me how.) Just type in the name of the person you're searching for, or their company, and cyberspace will supply you with an abundance of information, from an amazing variety of sources—glowing, damning, and everything in between.

For instance, what sort of training and background does your man have? What previous jobs did he hold? Is he well-respected in the industry? Is he well-liked by his own employees? Is he happily married, or a serial divorcee? Are there skeletons in his closet—bankruptcies, SEC investigations, accounting irregularities in companies he's run? Does he have a good sense of humor? Is he in good health? Does he cook?

Getting personal information about the company's people helps you "fill in the blanks" left by financial reports, no matter how complete they may be. For instance, a fifteen-minute Google search on John Chambers, CEO of Cisco Systems, produces a revealing snapshot of a gifted leader. You discover that he is widely respected for his visionary strategy, his ability to drive an entrepreneurial culture, and his warmhearted, straight-talking style. He joined Cisco in 1991 as senior vice president, after spending eight years at Wang

Laboratories and six years with IBM. He holds a J.D. degree and a B.S./B.A. degree in business from West Virginia University. Friends at his old alma mater, Indiana University (where he earned an M.B.A.), have chipped in $1.2 million to endow the John T. Chambers Chair in Internet Systems in his honor. He was named "Mr. Internet" by *Business Week* magazine in 1999, as well as being named one of the top twenty-five executives in the world for the second time in three years. ABC's *20/20* called him "The Best Boss in America." And so on.

This kind of personal information about a company's human DNA can be extremely valuable. Still, it's unwise to invest *only* on the strength of a single visionary leader, or even an entire management team. "When a management with a reputation for brilliance tackles a business with a reputation for poor fundamental economics," Warren Buffet has written, "it is the reputation of the business that stays intact." A company's people are just one part, though a very important part, of your total assessment of a stock.

Use the "PEG" ratio to find cheap, fast-growing stocks. Buy low, sell high.

That's the whole idea of making money in the stock market. Unfortunately, like everything else about the market, that's easier said than done. One problem is that often it's quite difficult to tell what's "low." When is a stock "cheap"? When is a good stock selling below its true value? How *do* you put a fair valuation on a company?

These questions are central to your search for good stocks, because buying stocks at a bargain increases your margin of safety and helps you maximize your profits if the stock takes off like you think it will. The quickest and most common way of getting a sense of how a stock's price compares to other stocks is the "price/earnings ratio," or P/E. A stock's P/E is listed on the financial pages of your newspaper next to the closing price of the stock. In effect, this number tells you how many dollars you're paying for each dollar of profits (earnings) the company is making. It's a way of comparing apples to apples—no matter what business the company happens to be engaged in, this is how much you're paying for each dollar of profits.

Historically, P/Es have ranged from around ten to around fifteen. That is, people have been willing to pay ten to fifteen bucks for each dollar of profits a company makes. (Actually, according to Jeremy Siegel, finance professor at the Wharton School, the average P/E for stocks since 1871 has been 13.6 percent.) In recent years, of course, P/E ratios have gone through the roof, especially for Internet companies—sometimes reaching two hundred or three hundred or even more. (Companies that have no earnings have no P/E. They just have a price.)

But in several ways, P/E ratios are a misleading way of judging the fairness or unfairness of a stock's price. Value investors tend to focus on buying stocks with a low P/E, but the trouble is that a stock with a P/E of eight is very likely to be that cheap for a reason. Bad stocks are always cheap; Microsoft has never been cheap.

For another thing, the P/E ratio is actually a look backward, into the earnings of the previous year. It's today's price relative to *last year's* earnings (or "trailing" earnings). It says something about the company's recent past, which is instructive, but it has much less to say about the company's future. (There is also something called a "forward P/E ratio," less commonly used, which tells you the price relative to the company's current fiscal year.)

There's no disputing the importance of earnings to a stock's long-term prospects. "An extraordinary long-run earnings growth rate is the single most important element contributing to the success of most stock investments," writes Burton Malkiel. "As difficult as the job may be, picking stocks whose earnings grow is the name of the game."

But when it comes to determining a reasonable price to pay for earnings, wouldn't it be better to ask, "Is this a fair price to pay for a company's *future* earnings?" After all, the past is past. What matters is the future, and over the long haul a company's earnings are the primary driving force for its stock price. If the company is going to increase profits at 25 percent a year, it's sure worth a lot more than a company that's going to increase profits at 15 percent a year. A stock selling at a P/E of thirty might actually be worth the price, because it has fabulous near-term earnings potential; a "cheap" stock selling at a P/E of nine might be overpriced because its near-term future looks dismal.

But how do you tell the difference?

That's where a devilishly clever little number called the "PEG ratio" comes in. Please bear with me on this one—it's the roughest math in this little book. But it's worth the trouble, because it helps you determine whether the price you're paying for a company's future growth is cheap, fair, or overpriced.

The PEG ratio is calculated by dividing a company's P/E into the projected future growth of its earnings. If a company has a P/E of fifteen, and the projected growth rate of its earnings for the next five years is 15 percent, then its PEG ratio is one. A PEG ratio of one is considered to be a fair price; you're paying just about the right amount for that stock. The basic idea is that a fairly priced stock would have a P/E ratio that is equal to its projected growth rate. A PEG ratio of, say, 0.5 is a genuine steal; in effect, you're getting the stock at half price. These are the sort of stocks that fund managers are constantly searching for—companies whose financial fundamentals are sound, but which have temporarily fallen out of favor with the mob. How does anybody know a company's future growth rate? Well, they don't. These projections are based on a consensus of earnings estimates by professional analysts. Being human, these people are smart but not infallible, so the further out the projections go—sometimes to five years—the less accurate they become. (Dr. Malkiel showed, in a massive study of nineteen respected securities firms, that their predictions for one- to five-year earnings were off by roughly 30 percent. "Financial forecasting," he concluded, "appears to be a science that makes astrology look respectable.")

Nevertheless, the PEG ratio is a nice, simple number that helps you find companies whose prospects are rosy, but whose price is still fair. It's a way of smooshing three important fundamentals—a stock's price, its growth rate, and its current earnings level—into one number.

How do you find out what analysts believe a company's projected earnings are going to be, and by extension its PEG ratio, without wearing out your pencil, your calculator, or your brain? Well, nowadays that's a cinch, especially if you have access to the Internet. For instance, if you go to the Excite home page on the

Internet (www.excite.com), and punch in the symbol for your favorite stock (say, Cisco Systems) under "Get Quotes," you'll find yourself face-to-face with a screen that's cram-packed with little blue hot links, each one a magic button that opens up another screen full of great stuff about Cisco. Click on "Analyst Ratings," and you'll get the best guesses of the forty analysts who follow the stock for the current quarter; next quarter; current fiscal year; and the next fiscal year. Click on "Fundamentals," and you'll find Cisco's PEG ratio along with its P/E ratio, dividend yield, earnings per share, one-, three-, and five-year revenue growth, and—who knows?—maybe even my grandmother's recipe for spaghetti bolognese.

The Value Line "timeliness" rank.

There are approximately seven trillion investment newsletters out there (I know; I must get junk mail from half of them), but the *Value Line Investment Survey* is the old reliable. And, you don't even have to buy it: it's available free at most public libraries. Warren Buffet, at a 1998 Berkshire Hathaway meeting, said of *Value Line*: "I don't know of any other system that's as good."

Value Line has devised a way to pack a phenomenal amount of information about a company onto a single page—things like a ten-year history of the stock's price, its splits (if any), earnings per share, and so forth. It's mostly numbers, which may not be your strong suit.

But, there's one number that's as ingenious as it is useful. In effect, it's a number that gives you a good sense of the viability of a seed you're considering planting in your money garden.

Every week, *Value Line* gives about seventeen hundred stocks a ranking of one (best) through five (worst). This "timeliness" ranking is an effort to squeeze a huge amount of information into a single number and predict the stock's probable market performance over the coming six to twelve months. A stock with a ranking of one is predicted to go up more (or go down less in a nasty market) than other stocks with a lower ranking. It's that simple.

Because it's been tested in the real, rough-and-tumble stock market over the past thirty-five years (having been around since 1965), this little number is worth its weight in gold. (Does a number have a weight?) It's not a perfect system, of course; nothing is. But, according to the company's records, if you'd bought a representative sample of stocks with a timeliness ranking of one back in April, 1965, and held those stocks for a full year, then updated your holdings a year later to refill your portfolio with one-ranked stocks, you'd have turned $10,000 into $2,132,900 between April 1965 and June 2000. That's a gain of 21,229 percent—twenty times better than the Dow Jones Industrial Average over the same period of time.

By contrast, if you'd had an evil, stupid twin who bought only stocks ranked five (worst) each year during the same period, a portfolio would have grown by a mere 147 percent.

So, it's worth a trip to the local library to check out the *Value Line* timeliness ranking of any stock that you're considering planting in your money garden. It's just a way of increasing your chances of growing something fabulous by fall.

The IBD "relative price strength" number.

Another really useful little number—another indicator of the viability of a seed—is the *Investor's Business Daily* "relative price strength" number. This ingenious, simple system was devised by William O'Neill, IBD's publisher. Like the *Value Line* timeliness rank, it boils an enormous amount of data into a single number, this time between ninety-nine (best) and one (worst). In effect, it sums up the price performance of a stock, relative to all other stocks, for the preceding year. If a stock has a relative price strength of eighty-five, for instance, during the preceding twelve months it outperformed 85 percent of all other stocks. Or, put another way, it's in the top 15 percent of all stocks. Which ain't too shabby. That means it's done well; it's got momentum. And though, as they always say, past performance is no guarantee of future returns, the fact is that as a general thing, a stock will tend to keep moving in the same direction that it's been moving unless there's something to stop it.

In other words, the IBD relative strength number gives you a picture of the stock's short-term past; the *Value Line* timeliness rank gives you a short-term prediction of its future.

How do you find a stock's relative price strength number? Just pick up a copy of *Investor's Business Daily*. It's listed right beside each stock in every issue.

More than likely, you'll be way ahead of the game if you try to pick stocks with a relative strength of ninety or better. (Don't forget, though: if a stock has a ranking of ninety or better, that also means it's been discovered by lots of other investors.)

Never stop learning.

The foregoing suggestions are not the be-all and end-all of stock investing, of course. They're just simple guidelines that—most of the time—have enormous power to help your portfolio grow. Even so, in the garden and in the stock market, there is always more to know and learn. And I'd like to end with a plea for life-long learning about investing—for a whole career devoted to working the soil, selecting seeds, setting them out, and watching them grow.

In the age of hyper speed and hypertext, of frenetic day trading and instant information, you get the general impression that anybody with a computer and a modem already knows enough to outfox the experts. I'm convinced that the amateur stock-picker can do very well indeed. But everyone, you and I included, can always learn more.

"When people ask me how to choose a good nursery, my answer is that they should go to the place where they get the best information," says Andre Viette. "What you're spending on a plant is often insignificant compared to the knowledge you're getting."

Agreed, Andre.

CHOOSE AN INVESTING STYLE THAT SUITS YOUR OWN PERSONAL MICROCLIMATE—YOUR "PSYCHOLOGICAL GARDENING ZONE."

"Gardening is not graceful, and it makes one hot; but, it is a blessed sort of work, and if Eve had had a spade in Paradise and had known what to do with it, we should not have had all that sad business of the apple."
—Countess von Arnim, *Elizabeth and her German Garden*, 1898.

Thumbing through the seed catalogues in March, every gardener has been tempted to order something really improbable and exotic to grow that season. I once bought a house from an old gardener in Allentown, Pennsylvania, and found evidence that he had succumbed to the allure of the outlandish: beside the front stoop there was a little edelweiss forlornly clinging to life, separated from its home in the Swiss Alps by quantum leaps of latitude and altitude. Each season, with great effort, it managed to succeed in producing a tiny yellow flower surrounded by a woolly, star-shaped bract. But, it never seemed happy in that place it clearly did not belong.

When I moved down to central Virginia, a mid-Atlantic state that is really only semi-southern (we're in gardening zone seven here), I couldn't resist trying to grow camellias. After all, I'd seen them growing in Georgia and even Williamsburg, which is only two hours away, so I planted a couple of waxy-leafed plants in a protected location. My little bushes put out a handful of tentative pink blooms, like shy girls, then perished in a hard frost after the second season. They just couldn't figure out how to be happy in this climate. I was also terribly tempted to try growing figs, after tasting some wonderful ones growing along a sunny south-facing wall at Monticello. I finally succeeded, but only after going to great lengths to shelter them from the winter wind and planting the hardiest varieties possible (hardy Chicago and brown turkey turned out to be the best).

Ultimately, though, most gardeners eventually discover that it's just not worth the fight to plant fussy, exotic species in their gardens. Once the tender forgiveness of spring is over, exotics just turn into an endless fight against everything that loves them too much—Japanese beetles, powdery mildew, mealy bugs, deer, root rot, the works.

Many plants are also so "site-specific" that you can plant them in a perfectly acceptable gardening zone, but because you planted them in the wrong place in your yard they just will not prosper. There's no overcoming a spot that is too shady, or soil that doesn't drain well, or soil that's too dry or too exposed. It doesn't matter how long you wait, you're just going to be fighting that place. On the other hand, I once planted a deep purple clematis beside my mailbox in Charlottesville and that plant has thrived so spectacularly it's become locally famous. Complete strangers would take a photograph of it and tuck the photo under my door. Or, they'd come to the door and say, "What *is* that? I want one of *those!*"

That's what happens when you plant something where it really, truly belongs.

And that's why, at the end of the day, it's almost always best to plant things that are suited to the soil, temperature, altitude, pests, rainfall, and frost dates of your gardening zone, and even the specifics of an individual spot in your yard. Planting things that actually belong where you plant them—unlike that edelweiss in Allentown—will save you a world of grief. Your plants will prosper with a minimum of effort because they are suited to the situation they find themselves in. Because they truly belong, your garden will be more beautiful, it will thrive with less effort, and you will get to spend more time in the hammock.

What could be better than that?

By now I hope you get my point: it's also critical to choose an investing style that suits your temperament— your "psychological gardening zone." There are as many ways to make money as there are ways to lose it, but the key thing is to find a method or technique that suits *you*—a method you can stick with over the long haul, a method that helps you meet your financial goals with a minimum of stress, a technique that suits your whole life—your tolerance for risk, dreams for your kids, commitments to charity, and desires—as comfortably as a pair of old goatskin gardening gloves.

For instance, people fond of dividing the world into two camps sometimes say that there are "stewers"—people inclined to mull everything to death—and there are "doers"—the action-oriented, Jean-Claude Van Dammes of the world. Well, for better and for worse, I've always been a "stewer." I've always had an almost limitless capacity for brooding and pondering, thinking and rethinking, hemming and hawing, revising, reexamining, and reconsidering, then taking in a little bit more information before I even lift a finger to do anything. Then, generally, I brood a little bit more.

To be truthful, I always felt slightly embarrassed about my natural-born dreamy slothfulness. I longed to be more decisive, more forceful and fistful and Jean-Claude–like.

What a revelation it was to discover that my laziness, love of learning, and slowness to act were actually terrific ways to make money in the stock market! Seemingly without effort, my innate temperament was helping me focus on deep, careful research, followed by years of doing nothing, which reduced trading costs and capital gains taxes at the same time as it helped me ride out short-term declines on the way to huge, long-term gains.

It wasn't even as if I consciously chose this strategy. It was just me being who I am. That's why it felt so effortless, so right—as it should be when you pick your own investing strategy.

It's important that your strategy resonate this deeply with your sense of self because it's something you should stick with at least as long, and probably longer, than a love affair. The great value investor Warren Buffet likes to say that the average investor should make only about twenty major investment decisions in a lifetime. Well, picking an investment strategy should involve only a couple of decisions over your lifetime. (Your strategy will no doubt change as your life and financial circumstances change.)

Another way of putting this was wryly summed up in a bumper sticker I love: "Bloom where you are planted." Understanding and accepting your financial circumstances is part of figuring out the best way to make your portfolio bud, blossom, and bear fruit.

Choosing an investment strategy that suits you depends on a number of things, such as your age, your overall financial goals, your time horizon, your liquidity and income requirements, and your taxes. But perhaps the most critical thing is your temperament, particularly your tolerance for risk. As one chagrined investor remarked, "You only learn your risk tolerance when you're losing money, not when you're making it!"

Warren Buffet's mentor, Benjamin Graham, once said that the memory of having been financially deprived twice in his lifetime made him embrace an investment approach that emphasized downside protection over upside potential. He had two rules, he said. The first: "Don't lose money." The second: "Don't forget the first." Temperamentally, this approach suited his whole life experience, so he became one of the canniest, carefulest investors who ever lived.

In this book, I have tended to emphasize an investing method that favors holding a relatively small number of diversified, individual stocks, counterbalanced by bonds, for a very, very long time. There are three reasons for that. Number one, it works (at least, most of the time). Number two, it's relatively simple. And, number three, it suits my temperament. I am by nature an optimist, and I'm young. (At least, I was young quite recently.) The idea of finding and holding great growth stocks is appealing to me because it suits my whole way of looking at things. I love it when something grows, whether it's my Intel stock or my bearded iris; this is something I can understand. Also, as a practical matter, most growth stocks pay little or no dividends, but I don't need the current income so I don't mind. This approach feels right to me. I can stick with it until I need a walker. (Of course, my bearded iris, no matter how beautiful, won't grow forever. There *does* come a time when it's best to dig up those depleted rhizomes and replace them with robust, young bulbs. The same is true of my Intel stock: there *does* come a time when it makes sense to sell. For more on that, see chapter 9.)

By contrast, the whole notion of shorting stocks (in effect, betting that they will go down) is entirely contrary to my temperament. I'm not arguing that you can't make money that way; you can. But to me, it's too clever by half. And, it's predicated on the perverse hope that a business will fail (or at least that its stock will fall out of favor). I just have no fundamental *feel* for this way of operating, and if you can't instinctively grasp something I don't believe you can ever really be good at it.

By the same token, I'm temperamentally unsuited to the frenetic activity that day traders love so well. I'm just too lazy and dreamy and absentminded for that. And, I don't care for the somnolent safety of tucking it all away in bank CDs or tax-free municipal bonds. Hedge funds? I'm too dim-witted to even understand what that means.

Investors, unlike plants, have a lot of flexibility in choosing an investing style. But, we can learn from plants nevertheless. British botanist Brian Capon, in a smart little book called *Botany for Gardeners*, explains that "in mute testimony to the persistence of genetic legacies, each [plant] species displays optimum growth only within certain precisely defined environmental limits, established long ago during ancestral evolution. No matter how many generations removed a plant may be from those ancient ties, it is generally 'programmed' to respond to a specific range of temperature and other climatic and soil conditions."

Plants, in other words, have virtually no choice about what they need to succeed. You, on the other hand, have a good deal of choice. Even so, you're temperamentally "programmed" to feel comfortable handling your investments in a certain way. It's best not to ignore that deep, underlying nature, whether managing your money or picking a life partner.

To be honest, I'm quite certain that other people, whose temperaments are entirely different from my own, have also been rewarded by the markets. For instance, there are times when the market rewards those whose nature it is to act quickly and decisively, those who thrive on action, risk, and adrenaline. (The success of momentum investors during the great bull run of the late 1990s comes to mind.) However, I must confess that I have little insight into that way of life. I'm a humble gardener, a slow person, and a dreamy devotee of blossoms and of bumblebees. I couldn't operate that way if I tried.

My point is simply that being true to your nature— whatever that may be—is the best way to succeed, in life and in investing. Because picking the right investment strategy is, in effect, a way of increasing your wealth simply by being who you are.

———

"The smallest sprout shows that there really is no death."
—Walt Whitman, "Song of Myself"

On March 16, 2000, the Dow Jones Industrial Average exploded, gaining just shy of 500 points on the day—its biggest single-day point gain ever.

"I'm dazzled," Byron Wein, chief market strategist for Morgan Stanley Dean Witter, told *The Washington Post*. Added Henry Cavanna, senior equity portfolio manager at J.P. Morgan Investment Management: "The market just erupted. It's one of the strongest positive market days I've ever seen."

Veteran market watchers were at a loss to explain this monstrous surge, since there was nothing in particular to trigger it. Alan Greenspan had not made any cryptic hints about the direction of interest rates. There were no mega-mergers announced, no earnings surprises, and no positive reports about the GDP or inflation. The market just seemed poised to explode, particularly the big blue chips of the so-called "old economy"—companies that make things like soap or dishwashers rather than dot-com dreams of one sort or another.

It so happened that my garden was also poised to explode. Pent energy was straining newly emerged buds; the grass, still bearing the grayish pallor of late winter, was prepared to begin manufacturing chlorophyll by the truckload. Then the sky darkened and we got a pounding of early spring rain that lasted all day and into the night. By morning the peach, cherry, and apple blossoms had burst into a frothing sea of pink and white. The Bradford pears were covered with white foam, like clouds. Forsythia, daffodils, hyacinth, flowering quince—they all seemed to have progressed three weeks in a matter of hours, as if the rain had actually sped up time.

And, in a way, it had, just the way the market had made a couple of months' worth of gains in a single trading session.

Well, that's the way the market behaves. That's the way the natural world behaves.

And that's one of the most valuable investing secrets I ever learned in my garden.

Here it is in a nutshell: "Stock gains tend to come in brief, intense bursts. Miss enough of them and you lose all the advantage of stock investing in the first place." That's the conclusion of a report from Sanford C. Bernstein & Co., a New York money management and research firm.

It's one of the delightful mysteries of the garden that living things also grow in "brief, intense bursts." There's that fabulous, almost supernatural surge of growth in the spring, followed by slower, steadier growth throughout the summer, followed by the harvest and the long, dark days of dormancy.

But as a gardener, the important thing for you to remember is that the only possible way to capture a plant's maximum growth potential is to plant a seed, water it, and just let the inexorable forces of nature take over. If you plant too late, you miss that fabulous growth spurt called spring. A more common problem is impatience: gardeners will plant something, then, if it doesn't thrive, they'll yank it out and plant something else. (This, in effect, is what thousands of investors actually do.) Come September you won't have much in your garden except a very tired and unhealthy looking tomato plant—probably without tomatoes.

By the same token, the only possible way to catch those brief, intense bursts in the stock market is to keep your money invested and just hang on for the ride. In fact, it's even *more* important for investors to keep their money invested than for gardeners to keep their seeds in the ground. That's because nature is at least reasonably predictable. You can pretty much predict that May is going to be a month of fabulous growth, while November will be a month of deceleration and dormancy.

But, short-term fluctuations in the stock market are virtually impossible to predict, and anybody who tries to do so is playing a fool's game. There will probably always be investors who try to "time" the market—get out before the market drops, get back in just before it rises—but, I've never heard of anyone who has successfully done this over any extended period of time. In fact, this is one of the central reasons why so many investors do so poorly.

Consider the following famous study by the market research firm Ibbotson Associates. If you average out all the gains in the stock market between 1926 and 1995, they found, it turns out that stocks returned a little less than 1 percent per month. But that's only an *average*. If you look more closely, you discover that most of that growth was concentrated in a very few months. Out of all those 840 months, there were sixty months during which the average return—in a *month*—was 12 percent. But, during all those other months—93 percent of the time—stocks were essentially flat. They just lay there, or they floundered about like beached fish, or they lost value.

The important thing to remember is that nobody can tell what's just over the horizon—a big burst of growth or a big burst of boring. And, the only way to overcome the uncertainty of the future is to simply keep your money in the market.

Another thing to consider is this: in one recent forty-year period, the market rose in twenty-six years, was essentially even in three, and declined in eleven years. This means that the odds are almost three to one against you if you're trying to "time" the market—be in cash when the market is going down, and in stocks when it's going up. In one study of all of this, professors Richard Woodward and Jess Chua of the University of Calgary determined that a market "timer" would have to be right 70 percent of the time in order to outperform a calm, steady buy-and-hold investor— a gardener—who simply planted robust seeds and just left them in the ground to grow.

If you don't think keeping your money invested makes a huge difference, consider that if you'd invested $1 in stocks in 1925 and done nothing but putter in your petunias, that buck would have grown to $1,114 (with dividends reinvested) by 1995. But investors who missed the thirty-five best months during this 840-month period would have seen $1 grow to only $10. In other words, *99 percent of the gains occurred in just four percent of the time.*

The only way that you can be sure to catch the growth spurt during that wet, sunny 4 percent of the time is to have a seed in the ground for the rest of the time. Besides, if you do this you'll have more peace of mind, and more time to putter in the garden.

Two finance professors at the University of California at Davis, Brad M. Barber and Terence

Odean, did a study that confirms the wisdom of the general principle of putting a seed in the ground and simply watching it grow. "Our central message," they conclude, "is that trading is hazardous to your wealth." They proved once again that Benjamin Graham, Warren Buffet's mentor—the sage of Omaha's sage—was right when he wrote fifty years ago, "The investor's chief problem—and even his worst enemy—is likely to be himself."

The Barber-Odean study, published in the *Journal of Finance*, tracked 64,715 household accounts at a large discount brokerage over five years (1991 to 1996). The bottom line: people who traded the most made far less money than those who traded the least. The high-volume traders had an average monthly turnover rate of 21.5 percent, and their returns were 11.4 percent annually. But, the people who basically sat on their hands—the gardeners—had a turnover rate of only 0.19 percent—and their annual returns were 18.5 percent.

Over time, these differences grow alarmingly large. The active traders, who had a turnover rate of almost 25 percent a month, kept an average stock for just 120 days. You can grow a dahlia in four months, but not a company.

For the active traders, $1,000 turned into $6,700 in twenty years. But for those who were wise enough to sit on their hands, $1,000 turns into $25,200.

Heavy traders, the study showed, were inclined to buy stocks that performed worse than the ones they just sold. And, of course, their trading gains were eaten away by an average of 4 percent commission fees.

This sort of behavior, they found, was amazingly common. In their study, the average family turned over more than 80 percent of its stock portfolio annually. That means they held their stocks, on average, for only about fifteen months.

The main reason for their poor performance, the authors reported, "is the cost of trading [and remember, these were discount brokerages] and the frequency of trading, not portfolio selection." And, they didn't even take into account taxes, which would have depleted actual gains even further.

The New York Stock Exchange reports that all this frenetic trading, though foolish, is actually becoming more common. In 1997, the turnover rate was 69 percent (meaning the average stock was held for seventeen months). In 1990, it was just 46 percent and in the 1950s, down in the teens. Turnover on the Nasdaq was even higher—199 percent, meaning the average stock was held only six months.

The experience of investors in mutual funds is quite similar. During one seven-year period in the 1990s, for instance, the Vanguard Index Trust-500 Portfolio, a giant with more than $50 billion in assets, averaged just a 5 percent turnover rate. If you'd put in $10,000 and added $100 a month for five years, you'd wind up with $37,961, according to the *Value Line Mutual Fund Survey*. During the same period, the same investment strategy in Fidelity Magellan fund (which has a turnover rate of 126 percent) would have delivered $31,820. That's 16 percent less.

As a slow person, a gardener, all this is quietly comforting news. It's a kind of sweet revenge against the testosterone-crazed, overaccelerated modern world. Because for us, it's easy to be intimidated by all those young guys in Armani suits with cell phones and beepers, working the trading floors on CNBC. The interesting thing is that they'd all probably do better if they sat under a tree and ate an apple rather than got on the phone and made trades.

(Don't forget, of course, that the whole vast multi-billion-dollar edifice of professional financial management would collapse if traders stopped trading. The Armani boys make money not by making you money, but by generating commissions by trading your money. Frenetic trading is not just a habit of mind, it's the institutional basis of the whole financial system.)

In fact, the best financial news show is not one you will ever see on CNBC. It would be run a full hour, and show nothing but wind on water, autumn light glistening through leaves, or goldfish drifting around in a pond.

In two other studies, professor Odean discovered another reason why madcap traders generally turn in such mediocre returns. It's because when traders decide to sell shares of a stock, the ones they buy "actually underperform those they sell." Why do they do this? It looks as though there's a familiar pattern at work: investors are especially likely to sell if a stock goes down, then regains a bit of ground. (Sound familiar?)

In general, Odean observes, investors are inclined to hold onto their losers because it makes them feel better for not having locked in a loss. There's always a chance the thing will recover—by acting as if there's still hope, you're minimizing regret. Then, if the stock recovers a bit, you feel better about selling it, even if you've lost money.

The entire foregoing scenario takes place in a person's heart, not their head. How many people work out their neuroses with their money in the market?

As Jerry Goodman (the financial journalist who writes under the pseudonym Adam Smith) has written, "If you don't know who you are, the stock market is an expensive place to find out!"

It's a whole lot cheaper, and more pleasant, to work out your neuroses in the garden. That way, at least you've got squash, melons, and tomatoes to show for your efforts.

SUMMERTIME

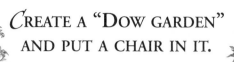

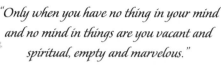

CREATE A "DOW GARDEN" AND PUT A CHAIR IN IT.

———

*"Only when you have no thing in your mind
and no mind in things are you vacant and
spiritual, empty and marvelous."*
—Zen master Te-shan/Tokusan

Once you've made your reasonably smart but not perfect investment picks, you come to the really, really hard part about the gardener's way of investing. What's that? Oh, nothing. Nothing at all. Because the real key to long-term success in the market is essentially a kind of *enlightened passivity*. As the great stock-picker Peter Lynch has written, "the key to making money in stocks is not to get scared out of them." That is, it's harder to avoid panic selling in a down market than it is to pick good stocks in the first place. That means you've just got to remember to do nothing at all.

Not as easy as it may sound.

In a famous little essay called "Three Ways to Succeed as an Investor," veteran money manager Charles D. Ellis argued that—well, big surprise—there are basically three ways to succeed as an investor. One way is intellectually difficult; one is physically difficult; and the third is emotionally difficult.

The first way is to be intellectually brilliant and have such a profound understanding of market forces and individual businesses that you see things before anybody else does. You're so far ahead of the pack that when you first buy a stock people generally think you're a fool. It's only in retrospect that ordinary mortals see what you saw. Only a very few people can consistently do this—financial Einsteins like Warren Buffet and Sir John Templeton come to mind.

I don't know about you, but frankly I'm not that smart.

Another way, easier though more physically demanding, is simply to work harder than everybody else. You read more books and reports, make more phone calls, burn more midnight oil, and generally just try to beat the competition by outworking it.

I don't know about you, but just thinking about this makes me tired.

The last way is the gardener's way—and it suits me just fine. You just figure out a long-term investment strategy that is right for you, make your investments, and hold on through thick and thin. Put your zucchini seeds in the ground, put a chair in your garden, and watch them grow. This method, says Ellis, "requires no great genius and no great brawn, but it works."

The great John Bogle, founder of the Vanguard Group of mutual funds, echoed this sentiment when he was asked what investors should do in the new era in which the S&P 500 stock index was more heavily weighted than ever by notoriously volatile technology issues.

"My rule has always been to do nothing," he said simply. "We say stay the course. But before you stay the course, make sure you're on the right course."

The big challenge is that it is emotionally difficult to do nothing, especially during down markets and droughts. Doing nothing is a whole lot harder than doing something. In fact, the relentless urge to do something—anything!—has probably gotten the human race into more trouble than any other urge. It's also depleted more portfolios than cocaine.

As a veteran money manager of an acquaintance once told me: "I spend more time managing my client's emotions than their money. Managing money is fairly simple. But, managing their expectations when the market soars, or their fears and panic when the market tanks—that's the hard part."

In down markets, brokers turn into therapists because the most critical thing for investors to do is...nothing. All they need is to have their hands held.

Sometimes that's the most important thing of all.

Consider this: during Peter Lynch's famous thirteen-year stretch managing Fidelity Magellan, the grand-daddy of all mutual funds, he compiled a record of 29 percent annual returns. That record is so amazing, and went on for so long, that it may never be matched.

(Lynch himself might not even be able to match it.) Here's something that's even more amazing: Lynch claims that most of the investors in his fund during his tenure actually *lost* money. How is that possible? They did not put their seeds in the ground and simply let them grow.

They jumped in and out. They bought the fund when it was soaring, or saw it ranked in *Money* magazine, then dumped it when it swooned a little.

Also, consider this: a Boston research firm, Dalbar Inc., looked into the restless-investor phenomenon a little more closely. They conducted a long-term study using a computer model to show how real-life investors actually fared with their mutual funds. From January 1, 1984, through December 31, 1997, the S&P 500 returned 820 percent. Here's the kicker: the average investor achieved returns of only 148 percent.

How come? "The gap is explained by the behavior of equity fund investors," the researchers concluded. "In their attempt to cash in on the impressive stock market gains, investors jump on the bandwagon too late, and switch in and out of funds trying to time the market. By not remaining invested for the entire period, they do not benefit from the majority of the equity market appreciation."

You'd think professional money managers would be a little bit savvier than that, but very often they make the same mistakes (and with more money—your money). The year 1998 was a successful year for stocks—the benchmark S&P 500 was up over 20 percent for the year. But, the average mutual barely broke 6 percent. How come? One key factor was turnover. Fund managers with suspenders covered with dollar signs were frenetically trading, trying to keep ahead of the S&P 500 and all their competitors with suspenders. Thus, they generated commissions for themselves (a cost to shareholders), charged you a fee for their frenetic services, and kept too much of their assets in cash between these trades, all of which reduced the returns to you.

You'd have been better off if they'd taken the day off—no, wait, the whole year!

Why is sloth such a reliable way to grow money and zucchini?

Because all this frantic, futile activity is very much akin to yanking out your basil when it's two inches high and planting nasturtiums, then yanking them out and planting leopard lilies. By the height of summer, you'd be exhausted and your garden would look pathetically shabby and rumpled. By contrast, your neighbor, who has spent most of August in a hammock reading *The New Yorker*, has a garden that's positively brimming with bloom.

It's unlikely that any of the aforementioned investors, amateur or professional, are any smarter than the brilliant billionaire Sir John Templeton, who racked up amazing 15 percent returns annually for thirty-eight years in his Templeton Growth Fund. Templeton finished at the top of his class at Yale and was a Rhodes scholar at Oxford. But, all those British brains didn't do him any good, he once observed, unless he was able to master his own emotions and thus keep from buying or selling when the best thing to do was nothing at all.

"Most investors get lead astray by emotions," he said. "They get excessively careless and optimistic when they have big profits. They get too cautious and pessimistic when they have big losses. I've always worked on having more self-control."

For Templeton, it's a powerful religious faith that seems to free him from the unsettling extremes of fear and greed. Convinced that "spiritual wealth is vastly more important than monetary wealth," his faith provides a calm, stabilizing center. (One of his investing maxims: "If you begin with prayer, you can think more clearly and make fewer stupid mistakes.")

Well, you may or may not be a religious person, but the gardener's attitude toward the stock market is really akin to that calm, long-term view that comes from faith in eternal life.

After all, every time you plunge your hands into the soil, or put a pumpkin seed in your palm, you are lay-ing hands on the eternal. The whole notion of doing nothing at all—no thought, no action, no mind—is also a religious idea, albeit a difficult one.

Yup: it's a whole lot like Zen.

So, I'd like to suggest a pleasant way to improve your success in the stock market while also mastering the art of doing nothing—a modest weekend project with both spiritual and financial rewards. Just set aside a part of your garden as a Zen garden—a "Dow garden," if you will—whose whole purpose is to create a calming, serene, harmonious environment, a place of rest in a stressful world where you can soothe your soul no matter what's happened in the markets that day. If the Dow dropped two hundred points, don't call your broker. Go out to your Dow garden, sit down in your chair, breathe deeply, and remember what matters.

Your Dow garden doesn't have to be much: in Japan, where there is an ancient reverence for the contemplative garden and space is at a premium, city dwellers create tiny gardens out of any available nook or cranny, even on a rooftop or a balcony.

In form and function, Zen gardens are actually quite different from the typical flower garden. They're not meant to excite the senses with extravagant bloom, with great varieties of form and color. Instead, they're meant to calm and soothe the soul. They're filled with understated elegance, a kind of quiet refinement.

Though they can take many forms, the whole idea is to create "soothing and reflective spaces that remain visually the same from one year to another," explains Sunniva Harte in her book *Zen Gardens*.

Perennial plants aren't usually grown in these gardens because their blooms are thought to be too transient. Instead, the Japanese love to use shrubs and small trees, rocks and gravel, which remain reassuringly familiar year after year. In fact, there are gardens in Japan which have retained their essential character for centuries. Zen gardeners delight in the notion that a favorite grove of trees or shrubs, or a certain mossy rock that delighted them as children, will still be there to delight their own children.

Now *that's* a long-term view, worthy of a successful investor—worthy even of Mr. Jefferson!

The whole process of designing your little Dow garden should be approached with a peaceful spirit. "The way the sun and moon travel around the garden is studied in order that everything, from the smallest plant to the largest rock, may be positioned in the most beneficial way," Harte writes of Zen-garden designers.

Your Dow garden should probably have a bit of water in it somewhere. The whole tradition of contemplative gardens grew out of the ancient Shinto religion, which revered all life. Since there can be no life without water, it was natural that a little pond or a waterfall would be a central element in most of their gardens. Even the smallest water feature, especially something that creates the sound of falling water, seems to soothe the soul and quiet the mind like nothing else.

But if water is too much trouble, there's also a Zen tradition of the dry garden, in which raked gravel or sand is made to look like flowing water, complete with rock "islands" that simulate a tiny ocean. Either way, investing in a little waterfall or a few bags of white sand might be the most useful thing you ever do for your portfolio.

Everything in the Dow garden should be arranged to create a scene that feels visually balanced and therefore calms the soul. It's good enough to do this by feel, just arranging things to suit yourself. Japanese and Chinese gardeners generally use the principles of feng shui, or geomancy, to help position things for maximum balance and harmony. The positioning of rocks, for instance, is considered a great art. To the Japanese, odd numbers (especially three, five, and seven) are equated with calmness and symmetry, so often plants or rocks will be grouped in odd numbers to create a space that feels gentle, spiritual, and unworldly.

By some irony, the ancient Chinese religious philosophy of the Tao (meaning "The Way") is pronounced *Dow*. And the Tao, or Taoism, refers to a kind of effortless action. A favorite analogy is to water: it is a lovely thing that flows without effort or resistance to the lowest level, yet it wears away the hardest substance. Following the way of the Tao means having tremendous power to shape one's life and destiny, while at the same time remaining deeply at rest and in harmony with the world. Taoists try to give up all striving, and through mystic contemplation attain a state that's completely free from desire.

Well, you're not entirely free of desire or you wouldn't be reading this book. (Hey, what's so bad about a little desire?) But, the analogy is powerful: attaining wealth in the turbulent financial markets also requires a kind of effortless action, an inner calm and simplicity. It's the sort of thing you can find only in a garden—a Dow garden.

But, even if you decide *not* to devote a special part of your garden to that purpose, you can simply consider your whole garden, just as it is, to be a "Dow garden," a place where you learn to master calm, patience, and doing almost nothing.

There are plenty of practical reasons why your garden is a good place to learn these lessons. Messing about with your plants is often as fruitless and wasteful as messing about with your stocks. Garden writer Henry Mitchell, in his book *The Essential Earthman*, complains about gardeners' inability to keep their hands to themselves at certain times of the year. Lilies are killed by the millions, he writes, because gardeners can't resist the urge to get out there in March to see if *L. auratum* is poking its head out of the ground. Because its stem wanders around underground like a snake and is therefore quite difficult to locate, "it is a very lucky auratum indeed that escapes being speared by an exploratory gardener." Spring bulbs like daffodils, hyacinth, and tulips are slaughtered in like manner, because gardeners can't resist fussing about under the leaves to see if the buds are coming up, and thus crush the tender little things.

What do you do if you fear the tulips will sprout too early or the lilies too late?

"One of the few ways I could really be helpful to any gardener is precisely at this point," Mitchell writes, "because this is something I know with every atom of bone and blood: don't do anything at all. Tulips come from some of the bleakest climates of this world—they have great powers of survival if left alone; but no plant has a chance if one wrong and disastrous thing is done, and that wrong way is invariably the way we gardeners choose."

This seems like a good moment to mention the seventeenth-century Dutch "tulipomania." (You knew I had to get around to it eventually in a book about gardening and investing!) Its relevance to the current discussion is simply this: keeping your head and doing nothing can be just as important when an "irrational exuberance" sweeps through the market as when the market heads sharply south.

Let what happened in Holland in the early 1600s be fair warning. Tulips—named for a Turkish word meaning "turban"—were first introduced into western Europe around 1550, and by 1634, "it was deemed a proof of bad taste in any man of fortune to be without a collection of them," according to Charles Mackay in his 1841 classic *Extraordinary Popular Delusions and the Madness of Crowds*. Gradually the passion for possessing these lovely, fragile flowers swept through every class of Dutch society, so that even clerks and shopkeepers began to compete with each other in the prices they paid for a choice bulb. Soon "the rage among the Dutch to possess them was so great that the ordinary industry of the country was neglected, and the population, even to its lowest dregs, embarked in the tulip trade."

Prices paid for coveted bulbs grew increasingly preposterous. Mackay records, incredulously, that somebody paid the following for a single root of the rare species called the viceroy: four fat oxen; eight fat swine; twelve fat sheep; two hogsheads [one hundred twenty-six gallons] of wine; four tons of beer; two tons of butter; two lasts [eight thousand pounds] of wheat; four lasts [sixteen thousand pounds] of rye;

one thousand pounds of cheese; a complete bed; a suit of clothes; and a silver drinking cup.

Eventually, the demand for tulips, especially rare species, grew so fevered that in 1636 a regular market for their purchase and sale was established on the Stock Exchange of Amsterdam and in other Dutch cities. "Tulip-jobbers" set to work at the ancient game of stock manipulation, bidding up the price and then selling. A mania for gambling in tulips swept over the country, and "everyone imagined that the passion for tulips would last forever, and that the wealthy from every part of the world would send to Holland and pay whatever prices were asked for them." Chimneysweeps and washerwomen converted everything they had to cash and invested it all in tulips. People sold their houses at incredibly low prices in order to invest in the tulip-mart. Trade in tulips became so complex and widespread that instead of notary publics, many towns had "tulip-notaries" to witness documents in the tulip trade.

Eventually, Mackay recounts, a few dim rays of reason began to shine through the mania, and "the more prudent began to see that this folly could not last forever...it was seen that somebody must lose fearfully in the end." Prices began to collapse. People defaulted on "tulip contracts," in which they'd agreed to pay such-and-such a price for a single bulb at some future date. People who'd sold everything found themselves holding a handful of tulip bulbs that nobody wanted to buy, even at a fraction of their cost, and "many a representative of a noble line saw the fortunes of his house ruined beyond redemption."

The mania for technology stocks that swept the U.S. stock exchanges in the late 1990s was often compared to the Dutch tulip craze.

(Though it wasn't a terribly apt analogy because technology will eventually revolutionize the world; but tulips, while beautiful, won't.) Still, manias and delusions will always sweep through the markets from time to time, and learning to stay calm and do nothing is generally the best defense against them.

In the garden, too, there's always a temptation to get swept up in a kind of mania—to overwater, over-fertilize, or just generally overfuss in your garden, any one of which can kill your plants. Swiss nurseryman Andre Viette likes to tell novice gardeners that one of the best ways to avoid fussing with your garden all the time is to avoid finicky plants.

Instead, fill your garden with tough, care-free, long-lived perennials—and your portfolio with sound, profitable stocks that will either pay dividends or grow capital gains, year in and year out. That way, you reduce your risk, you reduce your worry, and you increase the amount of time available for afternoon naps.

The wonderful thing about the gardener's way of investing is that after a brief period of intense activity (or at least, intense research), it rewards sloth. Warren Buffet, as usual, said it best. His own strategy, he's said, is to buy good companies at a decent price and then, when it comes to selling them, use "lethargy approaching sloth."

And, there is a perverse and quiet pleasure in being richly rewarded for doing absolutely nothing.

Keep in mind: you're not actually *running* this company you've invested in. (Now that *would* be work!) You're only loaning it a bit of money by buying its stock. You're not out finding new markets or managing inventory or squeezing costs or finding ways to widen the profit margin. You're not in control of inflation or the price of the yen against the dollar or any other macroeconomic force, either.

By the same token—unless you have serious psychiatric problems you're not telling people about—you are not *causing* the growth of this zucchini plant. You're only optimizing conditions so that it can grow itself. It knows perfectly well what to do without you.

As an investor, and a gardener, the only real way to make your zucchini grow faster is to simply ignore it until August.

There are really only two tasks you need to rouse yourself to perform in the summertime garden: weeding and watering. The main thing to remember about weeds, says Andre Viette, is this: don't let them get away from you. It's much easier to weed lightly and frequently than to fight the engulfing horde that will appear in your flowerbeds if you ignore them for weeks.

The biggest mistake most gardeners make is not understanding how to water properly, Andre says. People tend to water their gardens too frequently, and too shallowly. Many automatic watering systems create conditions that are almost like a tropical rain forest. The key, he says, is deep, infrequent watering. He suggests that, if you have sprinkling system, you should use nozzles that put out a gentle, rain-like spray rather than a heavy downpour. In the summer, he likes to get an inch to an inch and a half of moisture into his soil every ten days. "It will take between eight and nine hours and up to fifteen hours to get one inch of moisture into the soil."

"People say, 'Well if you water that long you'll get disease.'" Andre says. "No. What gives you disease is watering too often. Deep watering is the key. Water, and then don't do it again for ten days."

The same thing is true of monitoring your portfolio: do it deeply and infrequently. That's precisely the opposite of constant, shallow, fidgety fussing—day trading, basically.

You've got to keep an eye on your stocks to make sure that their story has not fundamentally changed, that quarterly earnings reports are favorable, and that there hasn't been a shift in the overall market that might have a negative impact on the company's prospects, and so forth. Almost always, though, it's best not to *do* anything. If you've picked good stocks in the first place, there is no need to check your portfolio three times a day. (I recently heard about a truly bad, truly twenty-first-century idea: a computer screensaver that displays your portfolio in real time, all day long.) It only makes you nervous, and more inclined to do something stupid. And, if you've planted robust plants that are suited to your soil and microclimate, they are probably far hardier, and less in need of human help, than most gardeners realize.

All this may sound like simplistic advice, and perhaps it is. I'm a fairly simplistic guy. I like simplistic advice. But, more importantly, if taken to heart, the do-nothing approach has absolutely phenomenal power to increase your wealth, just as the do-something approach has amazing power to piddle it away.

That's why it's both wise and pleasant to put a chair in your garden and just sit there, watching the plants grow. Unknowing rubes who do not garden are fond of saying, their tongues dripping with scorn, that in out-of-the-way towns, "there's nothing to do but watch the grass grow." Well, actually, watching the grass grow can be quite interesting. Especially if it's making you rich.

DROUGHTS ARE INEVITABLE—BUT EVENTUALLY, IT ALWAYS RAINS.

"There's a certain Buddhistic calm that comes from having ...money in the bank."
—Tom Robbins, *Even Cowgirls Get the Blues*

In the spring, the garden is filled with miracles. Plants surge forth, almost supernaturally green. Buds swell, shatter, and explode into bloom. The soil seems so fecund you almost imagine that a hoe, stuck in the ground, will begin leafing out in a matter of days. Your job as a gardener seems so easy! The Japanese beetles have not yet arrived; it rains almost every day; the vegetables are still outrunning the weeds; and, there's enough tender forage in the woods to keep the deer out of your cabbages.

It's so easy to stand there admiring your little plot of paradise thinking, "Man, am I a good gardener! I mean, really good!"

Then, the hammering heat of summer comes. The Japanese beetles arrive. The deer. The rabbits. The weeds. The drought.

Your squash and tomatoes huddle forlornly in the wilting shade of dry, cracked leaves.

Then, it's easy for you to stand there surveying your pathetic, failed experiment in plant husbandry saying, "This is ugly! This is awful! I quit!"

But, the main thing to remember about droughts, bad weather, and stock market slumps is this: they'll go away.

And, they will also come back again.

In fact, as Peter Lynch is fond of pointing out, over the past seventy years the stock market has declined more than forty times. And, it's going to do it again.

Understanding this simple truth in a deep, calm way—and not being panicked by it—is one of the most critical differences between successful and unsuccessful investors, and successful and unsuccessful gardeners.

For a little advice from a master, take a peek into Thomas Jefferson's famous *Garden Book*, a tattered leather-bound volume into which, for nearly sixty years, Mr. Jefferson made meticulous notes about the goings-on in his garden at Monticello. He recorded what he planted and when, the dates when vegetables came "to table," the extent of frost and drought damage to his and his neighbors' gardens, and the results of his experiments as a horticultural scientist and pleasure gardener.

On May 5, 1774, he placidly noted "a frost, which destroyed almost everything. It killed the wheat, rye, corn, many tobacco plants, and even large saplings. At Monticello near half the fruit of every kind was killed...this frost was general and equally destructive thro the whole country and the neighboring colonies."

It's easy to forget that Mr. Jefferson's gardens were not merely ornamental, or simply to supplement what he could buy at the local Jiffy Mart. His farm and garden had to feed an enormous household (including, unfortunately, more than one hundred slaves). Yet, Jefferson never makes any particular comment about this frost disaster except to precisely describe it. The next entry in the ledger, on May 14th, says simply, "cherries ripe."

Cherries ripe!

These are the words of a wise, calm, experienced gardener—someone who had lived through frosts and droughts and pest infestations, and knew he would again.

Mr. Jefferson's almost Buddha-like calm in the garden is the same calm you need to bring to the uncertain climate of the financial markets. It's not an easy lesson to learn: it's something it takes many growing seasons to master. (I'm still trying!)

In learning this hard lesson, gardeners have at least one psychological advantage over investors: even if they may not anticipate precisely when a spell of bad weather will come, at least they know that the growing season will be over by winter.

Investors, on the other hand—despite all the historical evidence to the contrary—keep being fooled into believing that winter will never come. Given a period of robust, year-on-year growth in the markets, they quickly come to believe that the growing season will never end. Such was the case in the latter half of the 1990s when the U.S. stock market experienced the longest sustained bull market in its history and investors began giddily expecting 20 or 30 percent annual returns as a matter of course.

Once you grow accustomed to these kinds of returns (and it's amazing how fast that happens!) anything less comes to seem like an unfortunate aberration. Actually, though, it's just a return to normal.

If you'd been paying attention to what's happening out in your garden, you'd know that.

John Bogle, the founder of the Vanguard group of mutual funds, once remarked that one of the most powerful forces at work in the market is "regression to the mean." Which means that, despite all its gut-churning ups and downs, eventually the market will return to something like its historic mean rate of return, which is a bit less than 10 percent a year.

Or, as Dean Mathey, former partner at Dillion Read, put it in an essay called "What I Learned from the Depression": "Extreme situations do not last, no matter what the apparent justification. No ladder is high enough to reach to Heaven. While we may have new 'eras,' old laws will still operate."

The trick is not to be misled by short-term financial events, buying in a rapture when the market climbs, or selling in a panic when the market tumbles.

Instead, remember the cherries in Mr. Jefferson's garden.

THREE KEYS TO CALM

Right research. The best way to stay calm in turbulent markets, of course, is to be stinking rich. On the off chance that you're not—that you really *do* need the money you have invested in equities—the next best thing is to feel entirely comfortable with your stock picks in the first place. (See chapter 2.) If you're convinced that your stocks are well-managed, profitable enterprises with a sustainable strategic advantage in a growing sector of the marketplace, and you're paying enough attention to them to know that their story has not fundamentally changed, why should you worry? Let other people worry.

Consider this comment from Larry Ellison, founder of Oracle and one of the world's richest men (perhaps, by the time you read this, *the* richest). In the fall of 2000, Oracle's stock price got hammered when the company announced that database sales would "only" grow a solid 15 percent to 25 percent in each of the next three quarters. At a meeting of analysts who follow Oracle, somebody asked Ellison what he thought of the decline in the stock price. He answered calmly, but with more than a touch of disdain. "First, I'm a man of modest needs and I can get by on my remaining $50 billion. Second, I have no idea what makes our stock go up or down—what you people do is a complete mystery to me."

In other words, he couldn't have cared less about the capricious, often foolish short-term fluctuations of the stock market, just as Mr. Jefferson was unruffled by a hard frost in that long-ago May. Both of them just carried on, keeping their eyes on the prize: one on building a world-class business, the other on building a world-class garden.

Diversification. The next most important safeguard to your sanity, in the garden and the markets, is diversification.

Princeton finance professor Burton Malkiel, in his classic investment book *A Random Walk Down Wall Street*, uses the following simple analogy to demonstrate how stock diversification reduces risk. Suppose there's an island economy with only two businesses. One is a resort with golf courses, swimming pools, and so on. The other is an umbrella manufacturer. Both of these businesses are dependent on the weather, but in opposite ways—when it rains, the umbrella-maker does well, when it shines, the resort does well.

Now (just to keep it neat and simple) suppose it's sunny half the time, and rainy half the time. And further suppose that, in the rainy season, an investor who bought stock in the umbrella-maker sees a 50 percent return on his money; when it's sunny, he loses 25 percent of his investment. But, for owners of stock in the resort, the return is exactly the opposite: 50 percent returns when the sun shines, a 25 percent loss when it rains.

The trouble is, nobody can tell whether it's going to rain or shine. So, though his average rate of return (or expected return) would be 12½ percent, he'd very likely have good years and bad years. His returns would be as volatile and unpredictable as the weather. However, if he took his money and diversified, putting a buck in the umbrella-maker and another buck in the resort, it wouldn't really matter what the weather did. If it rained, he'd make 12½ percent return; if the sun shone, he'd make 12½ percent. His returns would be that much more stable and predictable.

In this analogy, the key variable affecting both these businesses is the weather. And, more important, this variable affects each business in precisely the opposite way: sunshine helps one but hurts the other, and vice versa. (Statisticians would say these two companies had a "negative covariance.") This is the critical element to remember in putting together a truly diversified portfolio; you have to make sure that the companies you've chosen will not all be affected by the same variables in business (such as housing construction, interest rates, the price of gasoline, or whatever).

As a practical matter, of course, nothing is ever quite so simple. Stocks, like flocks of sheep, tend to move up or down together, especially stocks in the same or related market sectors. If the economy goes into recession, everybody gets nervous, people cut back on spending, and every business suffers, whether they make umbrellas or golf clubs. Still, diversification is one of the most venerable and best-documented ways to reduce your risk in the market.

How many stocks do you need to adequately diversify a portfolio? Probably fewer than you think. Holding any more than about twenty individual issues does little to decrease your risk; it just makes your life more complicated. It's important to remember, though, that those twenty core stocks need to be diversified among different market sectors. Even if you've invested a chunk of change in one market sector, it's a good idea to keep your investments diversified within that sector. For instance, if you wanted to put a chunk of change into technology stocks, you could spread your money into Dell (a computer retailer); Microsoft (software); America Online (online service); and Intel (chipmaker).

In fact, it's easy to get carried away with the notion of diversification. Investing in mutual funds seems to promise safety and stability because funds may invest in hundreds or thousands of different stocks in a whole variety of market sectors. How could you lose? But funds, besides reducing your returns by charging a fee for their services, often invest in so many companies that they virtually guarantee mediocre returns. The math is straightforward: how much more difficult would it be for five hundred companies to beat the market indexes than for twelve companies to do so?

"Over-diversification is probably the greatest enemy of portfolio performance," money manager Richard Jenrette said in a famous speech to the New York Society of Security Analysts. "Most of the portfolios we look at have too many names. As a result, the impact of a good idea is negligible...In our opinion, twenty-five to thirty companies is enough diversification even for a fund of $100 million. For a $1 million portfolio seeking to outperform the market, we believe the number of holdings might be as low as ten to fifteen. We have yet to find an institutional investor who had more than ten to fifteen investment ideas that he really liked at a given time."

Keeping your portfolio diversified, but not too diversified, enables you to get superior returns. It also enables you to monitor your holdings without spending your whole life reading the financial pages.

After all, it's possible to plant a hundred different vegetables in your garden, and in this way make absolutely certain that you'll foil at least most of the

aphids, loopers, and moths. But, who's got the time? And, if it's not necessary, why bother?

The mad scramble for diversification—which is essentially a quixotic search for absolute safety in the stock market—can be summed up by a simple fact: there are now more mutual funds (about eleven thousand) than there are publicly traded companies (about ten thousand). There have been more attempts to limit the risk in holding stocks than there are stocks themselves. Some brokerage houses now even offer "funds of funds," in which you may invest in a dozen different mutual funds, each of which is invested in hundreds of companies. At that rate, you might as well buy an "index fund," which mimics the performance of the market as a whole. (In fact, given how few professional money managers have been able to match the performance of the S&P 500 in recent years, that's not a bad idea.)

But there's something else that's even more important than diversifying your stock portfolio: it's called "asset allocation." That means making sure that *all* your investments are adequately diversified among all the different classes of assets (stocks, bonds, real estate, hog bellies, whatever). The term "asset allocation" has only been knocking around for the past thirty years or so, but it's hardly a new idea. In the Jewish holy book the Talmud, thought to have been written roughly two thousand years ago, there's this: "Let every man divide his money into three parts, and invest a third in land, a third in business, and a third let him keep in reserve."

That pretty much sums it up. It really matters: according to financial analyst Roger Ibbotson, who has intensively studied the returns from various portfolios, over 90 percent of an investor's return is based on asset allocation. Amazingly, less than 10 percent of an investor's return turns out to be the specific stocks or mutual funds you hold.

In tough times, though, it all gets a whole lot more personal than some abstract concept like "asset allocation." When the stock market tanks, I develop a great, sweet affection for my stodgy old tax-free municipal bonds. When August goes by without a drop of rain and my impatiens are wilting by noon, I practically get misty-eyed over my black-eyed Susans, real tough ladies who can produce buckets of bloom out of a rough, rocky hillside.

That's what diversification is all about: musical chairs of love.

The value of diversifying your holdings within reason, and the danger of not doing so, is almost precisely mirrored in the world of the farm and garden. Nature knows very well that maintaining a wide genetic diversity of plants provides a critical margin of safety against the enemy—pests, diseases, catastrophic drought, and all the other perils that can wipe out a species.

It's humans who seem to have forgotten this. Over the past century, there has been a huge loss of diversity in plants grown for human consumption all over the world. According to John Tuxill, of the Worldwatch Institute, there are 81 percent fewer tomato varieties grown in the United States today than there were before 1904. There are also 90 percent fewer kinds of peas and cabbages. In China, it's estimated that ten thousand varieties of wheat were grown in 1949, but only about one thousand by the 1970s.

Something we'd never allow in our personal portfolios, we've allowed in the world's gardens. (And let's face it: food is more important than money.)

The much-vaunted Green Revolution, which introduced high-yielding wheat, corn, rice, and other crops into the Third World, has been partly to blame for reducing the number of varieties of food crops that are grown worldwide. In one recent year, for instance, 67 percent of all the wheat grown in Bangladesh was the same, single variety. That's like putting 67 percent of all your money into one stock.

"The ecological risks we take in adopting such genetic uniformity are enormous," Tuxill writes. Why does this matter? It matters for the same reason that your stock portfolio should be distributed across a range of market sectors. It's a way of limiting the damage when disaster strikes.

And, you know that day will come.

Just ask Mr. Jefferson.

Temperament. There's a popular personal finance book called *The Unemotional Investor.* Well, you might call the book you're reading "*The Emotional Investor*"— not because I'm advocating buying stocks on a whim, but because I believe the emotional, psychological, temperamental side of investing is as important as P/E ratios or dividend yields (if not more so).

Picking an investment strategy that matches your lifestyle and life goals, making your investments, and then hanging on through thick and thin: that's more a question of *attitude*, and of temperament, than it is of financial acumen.

The challenge of keeping calm in the face of catastrophe or even uncertainty (which the CEO of AT&T once called "the hobgoblin and enemy of investment") is as tough for investors as it is for gardeners. Gardeners are inclined to overreact to reports of incoming bad weather, but investors are even worse. Since the stock market is forever trying to predict not only what's going to happen next but what other people *think* is going to happen next, investors are inclined to bail out not when a crash has happened, but when they think one is *about* to happen. They're trying to beat other investors to the emergency exit. By doing this, they are almost invariably worse off than they would have been if they'd just stayed calm and stayed put. As Peter Lynch once put it: "Far more money has been lost by investors preparing for corrections than has been lost in the corrections themselves."

Investors can learn a lot about how to survive in down markets by studying what plants do in dire circumstances like extreme heat, drought, or cold. Unlike some investors, plants don't assume that harsh conditions, however unpredictable, are an unfortunate anomaly or accident. Instead, they have an expectation of adversity built right into their cells. If they didn't, they wouldn't be here. Because countless generations of evolution—countless bull and bear markets, so to speak—have made them cunningly adapted to almost every bad thing that could possibly happen. They know it's coming; they just don't know when.

One thing that's critical to a plant's survival is regulating the uptake and release of water. Water that's drawn up through the roots by capillary action floods the plant's cells and is then "sweated" off through thousands of tiny pores in the leaves. But this is a flexible, adaptable system, ready to shift into survival mode if conditions get hazardous. On extremely dry or windy days, these pores or stomata will snap shut in order to conserve moisture. Desert plants have adapted to extremely dry conditions by only opening their pores at night, when water loss is reduced.

Plants can also regulate their own plumbing to avoid catastrophic damage in a freeze. The great danger is that if water freezes inside a plant's cells, the cell walls burst and the plant cannot survive. As nights get cooler, plants prepare for winter by "cold hardening."

The flow of water through their cells slows to a standstill. Dissolved sugars begin to accumulate within the cells, lowering the freezing point of water and acting like "antifreeze" to protect against freeze damage, just like the antifreeze that protects your car's cooling system in winter. Plants' cell walls also become more permeable, so that water can leak through into the intercellular spaces and thus avoid freeze damage.

In short, plants have all manner of ways in which they hunker down to survive, just as investors must learn to do when they're convinced they're holding good stocks in a bad market. In fact, plants have devised a kind of ultimate form of hunkering down: the seed. An annual will completely die off at the end of the season, but it always leaves a little pinch of its own DNA, wrapped in a tough husk, that will survive its parents death to bloom another day.

One of a seed's central survival tricks is dehydration. Less than 2 percent of a seed's weight is water, compared with about 95 percent water in a mature plant, according to British botanist Brian Capon, in his book *Botany for Gardeners*. It's this low water content that enables a seed to survive freezing temperatures that an adult plant could not—when water freezes inside cells, it bursts them apart. By keeping its cells dehydrated and dormant, these incredible little pods become space capsules afloat in time. They can wait out years of drought, like a patient investor awaiting the return of more favorable market conditions. In fact, ten thousand–year-old lupine seeds, deep-frozen in the arctic tundra, were successfully "brought back to life" and sprouted, writes Capon. Even seeds stored at room temperature can last an incredibly long time. Mimosa seeds stored for 221 years at the Natural History Museum in Paris burst into life after receiving a magical kiss of water.

Even the greatest investors don't know how to hunker down *that* well! Still, people who have been enormously successful in business invariably have the ability to remain largely unaffected by bear markets, the temperamental equivalent of plants' ability to survive a drought.

On February 18, 1999, after Internet and computer stocks went through one of their periodic swoons, Bloomberg reported that Bill Gates had suffered a paper loss of $14.6 billion dollars. His net worth, which topped out the year at $87.9 billion at its high, was down to a paltry $73 billion—a loss of 17 percent. Microsoft cofounder Paul Allen lost $4 billion; Dell

Computer's Michael Dell $4.9 billion; Amazon.com's Jeff Bezos $5.6 billion.

The main point to remember is this: these people are not worrying about these mostly imaginary losses. How can I tell? Because if they were, they wouldn't be that rich.

They've set their sights on a horizon far away. They've planted a garden so vast it will outlive them. That makes one little drought seem like nothing more than the shadow of a passing cloud.

YOU'RE A GARDENER, NOT A FARMER—SO GARDENING SHOULD BE A HOBBY, NOT A FULL-TIME PURSUIT.

"A gardener's work is never at an end; it begins with the year, and continues to the next: he prepares the ground, and then he sows it; after that he plants, and then he gathers the fruits..."
—John Evelyn, *Kalendarium Hortense*

On the one hand, you've got a backyard gardener who's planted enough tomatoes to make sandwiches for the summer and give a few away to friends and neighbors.

On the other, you've got a tomato agribusiness, supplying pizza chains and ketchup makers with tomatoes by the tanker truckload.

Despite the fact that the backyard gardener only has forty square feet of dirt and a few afternoons a week to work with, he's actually got a better chance of growing beautiful tomatoes than the big guy.

Sometimes it's hard to believe. But, it's something small gardeners—and small investors—all too often forget.

"Many people say that the individual investor has scarcely a chance today against Wall Street's pros," writes Burton Malkiel, in his classic investing book *A Random Walk Down Wall Street*. "Nothing could be further from the truth. You can do as well as the experts—perhaps even better."

Peter Lynch, the prince of common sense stock-picking, puts it more forcefully in his book *Beating the*

Street: "An amateur who devotes a small amount of study to companies in an industry he or she knows something about can outperform 95 percent of the paid experts who manage the mutual funds, plus have fun in doing it."

How is this possible?

Well, for one thing, the performance records of those vaunted experts is not really all that impressive, and hence not all that hard to beat. "Over the last decade, up to 75 percent of the equity funds have been worse than mediocre, failing to outgain the random baskets of stocks that make up the market indexes, year in and year out," observes Lynch.

By contrast, consider the record of the more than ten thousand amateur stock-picking clubs who are members of the National Association of Investors Corporation. Over the decade of the 1980s, these kitchen-table stock-picking clubs outperformed three-quarters of all professionally managed equity funds (as well as the S&P 500, a standard benchmark).

Why? Because the hobby investor has the same strategic advantages that the backyard gardener has over the professional farmer.

For one thing, the little guy doesn't have to grow seventy tons of tomatoes, only a nice shiny bushel or two—just enough to be pleasant and manageable and fun. All he's got to do is tend eight or ten plants, which is so few that he can simply pick the tomato horn-worms off by hand; hiring a cropduster would be a lit-tle laughable (and would probably irritate the neighbors).

By the same token, the small investor doesn't have to manage a billion dollars (or even five or ten), as many institutional money managers do. What a relief! Because with mindboggling amounts of money pour-ing in from investors each day (especially when the market is going up), professional fund managers are *forced* to invest in stocks, even if they don't have any really great ideas, and even if the timing is not ideal. Often there are institutional requirements that a cer-tain percent of assets must be invested in equities, so they have no choice. And, the Securities and Exchange Commission (SEC) also has a requirement that no holding in a mutual fund can exceed 5 per-cent of total assets. That means fund managers have to diversify into at least twenty issues (and usually far more). Again, money managers are *forced* to diversify, whether they want to or not, or whether it's a good idea or not.

The backyard tomato grower, by contrast, is not forced to do anything.

Professional money managers are also continuously under the gun to show great results at the end of each quarter, so that their fund will show up on lists of the

"hottest funds" and thus attract new business to their firms. This process, known as "window dressing," is a result of the intense competition throughout the financial services industry, and it has the effect of encouraging professionals to do things that the savvy amateur would never do. The professionals, in addition to being under pressure to show great total performance, are also under pressure to show investors that they've jumped on each quarters' hottest stocks, whether it be JDS Uniphase or Amgen. But, that's a truly nutty way to approach your investments. If you go out into the marketplace grabbing the quarter's "hot" stocks, only to show investors that you've got them in the portfolio, you're no longer looking for good investments. You're just looking for a stock that has smartly appreciated, which means that it's probably not a great buy. This business of madly switching from security to security in an attempt to catch the winners is the very reason so many investors, professional or amateur, often do so poorly.

By contrast, the small investor, tending his little tomato patch of stocks, isn't under any pressure to show anybody anything, or to prove anything to anyone. If you don't see anything worth buying out there, if you don't have any particularly great ideas, if you don't have any spare cash to invest—well, so what? It doesn't matter.

Just do nothing. That's your strategic advantage. And, more often than not, doing nothing is the best course of action.

Mutual funds also charge a fee for their services, of course. Which means that, instead of handing the capital gains and dividends on your stocks directly over to you, the fund takes a slice off of the top. In effect, they're raising the bar over which you've got to jump to match the market's performance. On the other hand, if you're just a hobby investor, managing a modest plot of individual issues yourself, you get to keep all those pre-tax profits yourself.

But, there's something else—something subtler, more metaphysical, more personal—that gives the leisure-time investor and the backyard gardener a special advantage. It comes down to this: if you approach investing as an enjoyable part-time hobby, rather than a full-time obsession, it keeps money in the proper perspective in your life—and helps prevent you from making dumb mistakes in down markets. If you allow your portfolio to occupy too large a place in your life, it becomes inherently unstable. You're too inclined to panic, to swoon, to sell or to buy, to just generally *mess* with the thing. But, if you're not turning to your investments as the source of all joy and meaning in your life, if you're just looking at them as a pleasant sideline, like playing chess or growing orchids, it's not like you lost your first-born son when the market tanks (as it is guaranteed to do at some point). You've just lost a little money. So what?

Thinking of your investments as a hobby means that, when the market goes south, it's easy enough to shift your attention to helping the kids with their homework or sanding your sailboat, rather than anxiously tracking the market on MSNBC. It's always easier to do *something* than *nothing*. Having a rich and interesting life in which your portfolio is just a part-time fancy is one of the best ways to hang in there for the long haul. And, that's the main trick of it.

But, what happens when people get overly fixated on the stock market has been played out in our nation's financial history over and over again. Wild volatility in the market is almost always accompanied by an unhealthy preoccupation with the market. In the late 1920s, just before the whole economy fell off a cliff, Joseph P. Kennedy is said to have gotten a stock tip from a shoeshine boy—and that's when he realized the market was so overheated it was time to sell. Whether or not this story is actually true, it makes the same point: obsessing over the market is inherently unhealthy.

Something similar began to happen during the great boom of the 1990s. In August, 1998, *The New York Times* reported that a cabbie had wireless Internet access installed in his cab to keep up with his stock portfolio.

FedEx deliverymen would check their holdings on a Palm Pilot while waiting for the elevator. A stockbroker of my acquaintance told me that among his clients was a doctor who would call to check on his stocks before going into the operating room for surgery.

This is not good for anybody—not the doctor's patients, or the cabbie's fares, or your portfolio, or the nation's economy.

This is about as far from enlightened passivity, from the gardener's way of investing, as you can get.

Of course, it's easy to retain an air of calm detachment when the market's doing fine. It's really hard to do it when it's not.

Such a moment came on August 30th, 1998, a gut-wrenching interlude during the long upward climb of the bull market. That day, the Dow dropped 512 points, about 6 percent, the second-biggest point drop in history. Over the preceding month, the Dow was down nearly 20 percent; the Nasdaq was even worse. Over $2.3 trillion disappeared from the capital markets in a matter of weeks.

At the time, I was holding (along with tax-free municipal bonds, a few mutual funds, and other, stodgier stocks like Fannie Mae and Berkshire Hathaway) five of the highest-flying technology stocks: Dell, Microsoft, Cisco Systems, AOL, and Intel. Though these holdings had vastly increased in value in the preceding couple of years, in the space of a month my "paper profits" fell back alarmingly. It's the sort of thing that tends to encourage people to believe they can fly right out a tenth-story window.

But, I had a curious reaction to all this. Since my portfolio was really nothing more than an interesting—though amazingly profitable—hobby, I was able to keep my equilibrium. In fact, those paper losses brought me back to Earth, to a renewed appreciation of what's real, and what matters. I came home after work that day and went swimming with my daughter. I laid in the pool staring up at the Maxfield Parrish cloudscapes and a few drifting nighthawks, a new moon rising over the hickory tree, and I thought: this matters. This isn't going to go away. The memories of this moment won't simply vaporize without leaving a trace, like capital gains have a way of doing.

The stock market can't make you happy—it only makes you money.

A daughter, or a new moon, or a tomato patch: now *that'll* make you happy.

℘RUDENT PRUNING
MAKES PLANTS PROSPER.

———

"Earths laughs in flowers."
—Ralph Waldo Emerson, *Hamatreya*

I'm back up on Monticello mountain again, sitting under a cherry tree in Thomas Jefferson's kitchen garden on a lovely early summer day. (Can't get enough of this place!) Today, I'm chatting with Mitch Van Yahres, a tree surgeon and arborist who has continued the work his father began here in the early 1920s, tending to the lovely old trees of Monticello. We're talking about the principles and practices of pruning—because pruning is as important to the health of your portfolio as it is to your shrubs and trees.

I'm especially interested in this subject because a couple of weeks ago a freak tornado packing eighty-mile-an-hour winds paid a tempestuous visit to my backyard, toppling a beloved old hickory tree we'd nicknamed Fred.

"Can you prune a tree to keep it from getting blown down in a storm?" I ask Mr. Van Yahres.

"Oh, sure—we do it all the time," he says. "Trees that have dense, packed-together branches tend to create a 'sail' effect in high wind. They'll just catch all that wind head on and it can take them down. So, we'll prune the branches to 'open out' the tree so that high winds can just pass through it. Also, by selective pruning you can improve the overall structure and stability of the tree."

If it's a fruit-bearing tree that you're working on, pruning has additional benefits. In his 1693 classic *The Compleat Gard'ner*—a book Mr. Jefferson might have owned himself—the French king's chief gardener Jean de La Quintinie wrote in his old-timey French way: "I will begin with the Reasons for which Pruning is used, which, in my Opinion, are two. The First, and chief, is, That which Pruning aims at, The speedy getting of abundance of fine and good Fruit; without which, no Fruit-Trees would be had, or cultivated. The Second, which is pretty considerable, informs us, that Pruning serves to make Trees, in all Seasons, even those in which they have neither Fruit nor Leaves, appear more agreeable to Sight."

Pruning also involves trimming out unwanted or unhealthy plant growth to benefit the living part of the plant, according to the venerable *Encyclopedia of Organic Gardening*, my copy of which is spattered with muddy thumbprints and faint brushstrokes of blood.

Dead and decaying branches are a danger to the whole plant, because they can allow rot to spread into the trunk itself and endanger the whole tree. To stimulate a plant's growth and production of "fine Fruit," to increase its overall symmetry and stability so as to survive high winds, to remove dead or decaying branches to protect the living ones, that's pretty much exactly what you do when you prune a portfolio.

Regularly pruning your portfolio is important because of a key wealth-building principle called "asset allocation." Asset allocation simply means the way you've spread your money over *all* the different classes of assets—stocks, bonds, cash, collectibles, real estate, hog bellies, whatever (as mentioned earlier). It's the principle of diversification applied to every kind of investment, not just stocks. It means not putting all your eggs in one basket. Or, more appropriately, not filling your entire garden with broccoli. According to financial analyst Roger Ibbotson, who has intensively studied the returns from various portfolios, more than 90 percent of an investor's return is based on asset allocation. Amazingly, less than 10 percent of an investor's return turns out to be the specific stocks or mutual funds you hold.

That's pretty incredible!

It means that you'd do well if, from time to time, you stepped way, way back from your "money tree" so that you could get a good look at it, top to bottom.

The whole question of how much of your assets you should have in each kind of investment is a complex one, having to do mainly with your age, aversion to risk, and net worth. But, it's important enough that it might be worth hiring a financial adviser to help you figure it out. One general rule of thumb is this: take 100 and subtract your age. The resulting number is roughly the percentage of exposure to equities you should have in your portfolio. That is, if you're 40, you should have around 60 percent of your liquid assets in the market; if you're 60, only 40 percent. As a general thing, the older you get the more you should shift your assets into less volatile investments like bonds, because you have less time to recover if the stock market takes a dive. A simpler but more telling indicator is the "sleep/deep" test: if you've got so much money in the market that you can't sleep, you're in too deep.

Peter Lynch recommends giving your portfolio this kind of checkup every six months. That doesn't necessarily mean actually pruning, just looking the whole portfolio over to see if any adjustments need to be made. Some stocks may have slipped in value, and if you feel they're still attractive businesses you might want to add to your position and thus "average down" your cost. Or, the opposite might have happened: a stock might have appreciated smartly, thus altering the asset allocation you'd originally planned. Or, you might notice a side-sprout or "sucker" growing out of the trunk that's just draining off energy from the tree—a worthless or middling or just irrelevant investment that would be better lopped off.

Typically, money managers consider only liquid or semi-liquid assets—mainly stocks, bonds, and cash—to be the important parts of the asset allocation equation. Because your house is not really a liquid asset, it's usually not considered part of the mix. But there's no need to get technical—the whole point is just to take a look at the big picture from time to time and do a little judicious clipping if need be.

The general idea is that you want to have *something* in your portfolio that's appreciating at all times, because conditions in the larger economy are always shifting, like the weather or the wind. When inflation is high, your real estate tends to appreciate in value but your stocks don't do so well. When inflation is low, stocks and bonds tend to do well but real estate, collectibles, and foreign stocks tend to do poorly.

If you've got your money tree properly pruned, straddling all these possibilities in a great, symmetrical bower of branches—well, you're safe as you'll ever be in an unsafe world.

Like pruning your portfolio, tidying up your garden with a pair of pruning shears can be a pleasant, almost meditative task, along with being a very useful and productive one. Prune it right, and the plant prospers, light and air is admitted to the interior spaces, borer-damaged stems are cut away, and a flower or fruit emerges like an apparition from the clean, diagonal cut.

It's a wonderful thing, really—like being a husbandman in the orchard of the Lord.

But, there's also a wrong way to prune a portfolio or a tree—sometimes, a *really* wrong way. People will do horrifying things to trees, like those hideous hatchet jobs where they basically lop off every limb to a distance of eight or ten feet, leaving a pathetic pincushion plunked at the top of a trunk.

"Why on Earth do people do this?" I asked Mr. Van Yahres.

"They do it because of ignorance, and because they're afraid of limbs falling down on the house, I suppose. But actually, that kind of pruning has exactly the opposite effect. When the shoots grow back in at the point where the limb was cut, they're much weaker, and much more likely to break off than they would have been if nobody had touched them in the first place."

As every gardener knows, there is a right way and a wrong way to prune a rose. There is also a right time and a wrong time to prune a rose. Actually, how and when you prune a plant depends on the kind of plant you're pruning, and what you're trying to achieve. But, as a general thing, pruning trees in summer favors flower and fruit production; pruning in winter stimulates leaf and branch production, according to the venerable old *Wise Garden Encyclopedia*, first published in 1936. Trees and shrubs pruned while they're dormant strive to replace the parts that were removed with new ones. The result is the forced development not only of flower buds but also of leaf and shoot buds that would otherwise have remained dormant.

It might seem that pruning a tree or a shrub is kind of unnatural. After all, who pruned the world before humans got here? But the whole process of pruning and renewal is something that trees and plants will actually do themselves if you're not around to do it for them. After a very dry August, the willow oaks and sycamores around my house began shedding leaves in order to protect themselves. Suffusing that entire leaf surface with water was putting too much of a strain on the tree's very survival, so the trees shed the burden.

Thought of another way, you could say that the trees were protecting their "core holdings," by divesting of inessential, unproductive assets that could drag the whole portfolio down.

Nature also prunes trees and shrubs through windstorms, ice, and overloads of fruit. But, it tends to be a little haphazard. Human pruning is a bit of an improvement over nature because it involves a thoughtful and deliberate removal of badly placed branches to increase the structural strength or architecture of the whole tree. And, a clean wound made by a pruning saw speeds healing and minimizes the risk of infection, unlike the jagged tears left by a windstorm. Overall, the hand of man is a little more efficient than a storm in stimulating the growth, balance, and beauty of a plant.

I thought of all these principles of pruning recently when an upcoming tax bill forced me to do a pretty serious pruning job on my portfolio. My ultimate goal was this: rebalance and stabilize the whole thing, reduce my risk, trim away assets that were either under-performing "suckers" or overperforming assets that had grown so large they were way out of proportion to the whole "money tree."

I sat down with my money guru, Peter Dawyot, and we took a look at our family portfolio of stocks, munici-pal bonds, mutual funds, and money funds. I also pro-vided him with a broad, simple outline of all our other assets, including real estate, collectibles, cars, and so forth.

The first thing that struck me was that my America Online stock had appreciated so madly over the previ-ous couple of years that it was like a gangly, fruit-laden branch weighing down one side of the tree. Although originally it had been nicely balanced with all our other assets, it had now grown so far out of proportion with the rest of the tree that it might simply snap off in a high wind and endanger the whole tree. Microsoft, also, had vastly appreciated, giving a lopsided look to *its* side of the tree. We decided to lop off the AOL branch pretty severely. Then we lopped off the Microsoft branch a little less severely.

Unfortunately, well over 90 percent of the value of my AOL stock was capital gains, so I'd have a whopper of a capital gains tax bill to pay. (That's the downside of success in the market.) In order to offset the taxes on those gains, I also sold off my stake in Whole Foods Markets, which had gotten a bit of a haircut (though the loss was only a fraction of my gains in AOL). We also sold off my stake in the Clipper Fund. This venerable value fund, managed by the astute James Gipson, of Beverly Hills, had very nearly matched the S&P 500 over the past ten years—a record very few fund managers could equal. But it had also begun adding to a small position in Phillip Morris, and this had made me feel increasingly uncomfortable—not for financial reasons but ethical ones.

Like everything else having to do with money, pruning a portfolio properly is not only about money; it's also about your emotions, your values, and your life. When we were through, though the portfolio was smaller, I felt better about it. It was better balanced and more stable. It could better withstand high wind, drought, or even an ice storm. We had shed an asset that made me uneasy. Our asset allocation was now closer to what we felt was prudent. And, of course, the tax bill was paid!

I felt pretty certain that come summer, we'd have a crop of peaches that would make even Mr. Jefferson proud.

AUTUMN AND HARVEST

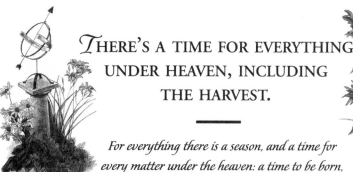

THERE'S A TIME FOR EVERYTHING UNDER HEAVEN, INCLUDING THE HARVEST.

For everything there is a season, and a time for every matter under the heaven: a time to be born, and a time to die; a time to plant, and a time to pluck up what is planted..."
—Ecclesiastes 3:1

Eventually, of course, there comes a day when you'll want to harvest your beans, melons, and corn. Hey, what's the point of having a vegetable garden if you can't make a tomato sandwich now and then?

Still, the harvest should not be the sole focus of your efforts in the garden. The *garden itself* should be your primary focus. Tending the soil, planting the seed, weeding, and watering, leaning on your hoe to survey your handiwork—that should be your primary pleasure and purpose in the garden, just as it should be in your portfolio.

Your garden, like your portfolio, should be thought of as something that's perpetual, that goes on bearing season after season, year after year. This season's crop is delightful, but it's the garden itself that lasts and lasts and lasts. Short-term expedients may produce a bumper crop this fall, but it may also do long-term damage to the soil. A successful garden and a productive portfolio both contain the element of longevity, of long-lastingness—even, you might say, of life beyond death, since both your garden and your money, properly attended to, should outlast you.

That's the way Warren Buffet approaches his own, rather splendiferous money garden. "When Charlie [Munger] and I buy common stocks...we approach the transaction as if we were buying into a private business," he's written. "We look at the economic prospects of the business, the people in charge of running it, and the price we must pay. We do not have in mind any time or price for sale. Indeed, we are willing to hold a stock indefinitely so long as we expect the business to increase in intrinsic value at a satisfactory rate."

In other words, he puts far more focus on preparing the soil, planting the seed, and watering than he does on the harvest.

Even so, there *is* a time to pick the pumpkin off of the vine. It's as foolish to allow your melons to ripen until they turn to mush as it is to ride your shares in the Eastern Buggy Whip Company all the way down to zero. How do you know when your crop is ripe for the harvest, or it's time to sell your stock? Here are five good reasons to "pluck up what is planted."

FIVE REASONS TO HARVEST THE CROP

The company is showing its age.

All the plants, trees, and shrubs in your yard and

garden have life cycles. Seeds have an extremely high mortality rate, but some eventually find fertile ground and take hold.

They germinate, and there's a period of frantic, almost miraculous growth, an outpouring of leaves and roots and shoots and blooms. Then the plant's growth rate begins to slow and it settles into maturity, shifting its energies into the production of fruit and seed for the next generation. Finally, it slips into a period of decline, decay, and death.

Even plants called "perennials" don't grow perennially; by definition, they simply grow more than two years. Some perennials (like delphiniums, columbine, and lupines) have fairly short lives, losing vigor after three to five years. Other perennials, like peonies, are virtual Methuselahs of the plant world; a good bed can go on gracing your May with feather-puff blooms for fifty years or more. Daylilies are also amazingly long-lived, and if regularly divided can bloom for twenty or thirty years, according to Andre Viette. But even these rugged bloomers eventually begin to show signs of age, losing vigor and petering out. (You can tell a daylily bed is aging when the flowers start getting smaller, Andre says.)

Pretty much the same thing is true of companies. The infant mortality rate is exceedingly high (especially, most recently, among high-tech start-ups); the survivors

experience a period of robust, often astonishing growth; then, there's a period of slowing growth, maturity, and decline. A raspberry bush doesn't live forever, and neither does a business.

Business Week magazine recently reported that in 1969 the five biggest companies in the United States (by market value) were, in order, IBM; AT&T; General Motors; Eastman Kodak; and Exxon. Thirty years later, in 1999, only one of them (Exxon, now morphed into Exxon Mobil) made the top-five list. The others had faded in the stretch, giving way to younger, faster-growing upstarts. By 1999, the four other biggest companies, in order, were Microsoft (which didn't even exist in 1969, Bill Gates being a pimply fourteen-year-old); General Electric; Cisco Systems (another company that did not exist 30 years earlier); and Wal-Mart, which in 1969 was all of seven years old, an itty-bitty five-and-dime little-known outside of Arkansas.

(In the age of Internet time, the life cycle of many companies—at least successful ones—has been vastly accelerated. Infant mortality rates are higher, but companies that survive infancy often grow at an astounding rate—a development filled with both risk and promise for investors. A mere seventeen years after it was founded (in 1984) by a couple of professors at Stanford University, Cisco Systems was the world leader in networking for the Internet, employed over thirty-four thousand people in 115 countries, and was capitalized at around $284 billion.)

If you go back even further, the story of corporate life cycles becomes even starker. Among the leading corporations in the United States a century ago were (no kidding) the Eastern Buggy Whip Company; La Crosse and Minnesota Steam Packet Company; and the Savanna and St. Paul Steamboat Line. None of them exist anymore (even though they all made their stockholders plenty of money in their younger days).

The take-home lesson of this story is that the fantastic growth rates of a young, robust company or industry cannot be sustained indefinitely. Or, as stockbrokers are so fond of saying, "trees don't grow to the sky." The trick is to buy stocks when they're still growing smartly, but consider selling them when their growth rates have slowed or grown stagnant.

If I'd been smart enough to invest $10,000 in Cisco Systems ten years ago (in January, 1991), my investment would now be worth $2,592,000—an increase of 25,820 percent. (These awe-inspiring numbers were churned out by a nifty little stock-price calculator on Cisco's website, listed under Investor Relations.) But, durn it, I wasn't that smart. Instead, I didn't start buying Cisco until 1997 and have "only" tripled my money since then. The incredible, unsustainable growth rate of Cisco's early days has no doubt passed; its growth rate has grown slower, steadier, and creakier with age (like me). Cisco is undergoing a kind of natural corporate aging process.

Part of this slowing growth has to do with a practical problem: the bigger a company gets, the harder it is to grow earnings at the same percentage rate as it did when it was younger and smaller. A company with $20 million in earnings needs to increase its profits by only $2 million to chalk up a 10 percent growth rate. But, a company with $100 million in earnings has to rake in an additional $10 million to hit 10 percent.

It's gotten overpriced.

One of the best reasons to sell a stock is if it's appreciated in value so much that you now feel it's overpriced. In effect, you should pick the melon before you think it's gotten overripe.

It's easy to tell if a honeydew is starting to get soggy, but how do you tell if a stock is overpriced? This is actually an exceedingly difficult question. Here are a few simple guidelines that may help. As a general rule of thumb, a fairly priced stock should sell at or below its growth rate (the rate at which its earnings increase every year). For instance, if your stock is selling at a price-earnings ratio (P/E) of twenty, and it's growing its earnings at a robust 23 percent annually, that's a square deal. You're actually buying those earnings at a bit of a discount. If, by contrast, a stock's P/E has sailed up to fifty (a dizzying level, considering that the historical average is around fourteen), and its earnings are only growing 18 percent a year—well, you're probably paying too much. ("Probably" because stock-picking is part art, part science. You may feel that the stock's long-term prospects justify its high price, and you may be right. That's what makes the market so interesting.)

If you look up your stock in the *Value Line Investment Survey* at the local library, you'll also find something called its "relative P/E." That means a number that shows how it compares to all the other stocks followed by *Value Line* (in other words, practically all of them). If your stock has a relative P/E of one or below, that means it's equal to or cheaper than the median price of all other stocks. If it's above one, that means it's more expensive. If you have a big position in a good company that's done exceedingly well, it's not necessary to sell off your whole stake. But, you might consider taking some of the money off of the table. Cisco Systems has been one of the fabulous growers in recent memory, but in early 2001 it was selling at ninety times earnings, which is steep even for one of the greatest companies on earth. Now might be a good moment to cut back your position in Cisco—particularly if you have a better investment in mind, or if you have done more research.

Of course, taking money off of the table when there still appears to be money to be made is one of the many things in life that's easier said than done. One of Sir John Templeton's famous investing maxims is that "the time of maximum pessimism is the best time to buy, and the time of maximum optimism is the best time to sell." However, another one of his maxims is a caveat: "To buy when others are despondently selling and to sell when others are greedily buying requires the greatest fortitude, even while offering the greatest reward."

This is probably the toughest lesson you'll ever learn as an investor—and the most valuable.

The story has changed.

In April of 1994, I bought a small stake in Telefonos de Mexico (TelMex), Mexico's national telephone system. According to my research, the company had a near-monopoly in a critical industry in a fast-growing economy—a sustainable strategic advantage in a trend that seemed likely to continue for at least three to five years. Though the stock had appreciated madly in recent years, it still seemed fairly priced, given its tremendous growth rate. One of the financial magazines was touting it as "the best stock in the world," and even Peter Lynch had taken a position in the stock (though, I realized later, he'd gotten in years earlier than I did). I couldn't miss, right? I bought the stock at 59⅜; it rapidly ran up to 62.

Then the story changed. AT&T announced it was making a major deal with a Mexican telephone company—but not with TelMex. An upstart competitor had just rudely crashed TelMex's "near-monopoly" party. Then the Mexican government devalued the peso, dealing the country's entire economy a serious blow. TelMex tottered and began to fall. Eight months after I bought in I bailed out, selling off my shares at $38.

Well, *c'est la vie*. Stuff happens. The important thing—in fact, your main research job as a long-term investor—is to keep an eye out for changes in your stock's story line. When the plot takes a turn for the worse, it's time to take your losses and get out.

You need the lettuce.

Sometimes, obviously, you just need the money. When you do sell something, though, it's important to take the opportunity to "prune" your portfolio wisely, making sure that you're keeping the whole thing balanced and stable, with all your assets allocated deliberately, like a well-trimmed tree. (See chapter 8.)

It's also important to consider the tax consequences of selling. When you sell a stock that's racked up impressive capital gains, it's a good idea to offset that gain by selling off your losers. According to current U.S. tax law, you can use your capital losses to wipe out your capital gains, dollar for dollar, up to an unlimited amount. (The tax code, of course, is just trying to make you feel better.)

The tax consequence of selling also highlights one big advantage of owning individual stocks over mutual funds. With an individual issue, you don't pay a penny in capital gains taxes until you sell it—thus giving you a great deal of control over the timing of your tax bill (though perhaps not the amount). But, mutual funds incur capital gains taxes more-or-less continually, because of ongoing selling (and buying) of shares in the fund. (You can even get hit with taxes that were incurred *before* you bought into the fund.)

In fact, "taxes can be the most significant cost of investing in a mutual fund," according to Paul Roye, director of the Securities and Exchange Commission's division of investment management. The amazing thing is that—at least as of this writing, in 2001— those mutual fund performance figures you read in the paper factor in the fund managers' fees but *not* the taxes you'll pay on dividends and capital gains. This is really significant, because taxes shave off *more than 2.5 percentage points* of the average stock fund's total return, according to the SEC. You may think your fund gained 12 percent last year, but actually it didn't even break ten percent. (Pending legislation may soon force mutual funds to reveal these truer numbers to investors.)

You were, uh, wrong.

It's absolutely guaranteed that you'll make some mistakes—maybe quite a few. Don't sweat it. If you become convinced that a stock you bought is a dog, hold it long enough to be certain it won't come back to life and then dump it, and do it without regret, guilt, or a backward glance. The worst thing you can do is to agonize over it.

"Buyer's remorse is a well-documented phenomenon in consumer markets, but it pales in comparison to seller's remorse: I sold too early; I sold too late; I should have sold; I shouldn't have sold," write Geoffrey Morse, Paul Johnson, and Tom Kippola in their bestselling book about technology investing called *The Gorilla Game*.

But fuggedaboutit. What's new about screwing up? You've done it before and you'll do it again.

"I must admit to being wrong perhaps about 20 percent of the time over a long period which totals to an awful lot of losses. However, it was the 80 percent that mattered," veteran investor Roy Neuberger has written with a sort of literary sigh. "One needs to recognize as quickly as possible an error in judgement...All in all, the essence of taking losses, which is ultimately a question of character, is to acknowledge when one is wrong."

Humility, after all, is a good thing, not a bad thing. In fact, it's one of the tastiest, most life-sustaining crops you'll harvest in the stock market. Or in your garden.

DON'T EAT YOUR SEED CORN.

"To own a bit of ground, to scratch it with a hoe, to plant seeds, and watch the renewal of life—this is the commonest delight of the race and the most satisfactory thing a man can do."
—Charles Dudley Warner, *My Summer in the Garden*

This book, of course, is about investing lessons learned in a garden. But, for this particular lesson I want to go way, way back, back to the days before gardens were merely a weekend pastime, back when everybody was a farmer, and every farm had to support a family. Back to the days when drought or pestilence or shortsightedness or plain bad luck could put the survival of a family, or a whole community, at risk.

In those days, at harvest time, people reaped the ripened vegetables and fruits and grains that they had grown. But, they also made certain to lay aside sacks of seeds for the following season. If they neglected to do this critical task, they would have nothing to plant come spring. (This was long ago, remember, long before the Burpee seed catalogue or Mr. Burpee; you couldn't just pop down to the local garden center in May and buy packets of carrot or cucumber or pumpkin seeds to make up for last fall's foolishness.)

Sometimes, of course, the harvest was poor and the prospect of winter grim. Even so, people had to resist the temptation to devour the entire crop, seeds and all. Because if they did, they'd have had to start the next year's garden all over again from scratch—begging, borrowing, or stealing seeds from somewhere, if they could find any at all. Rather than capitalizing on the efforts of previous seasons by starting the season with a sackful of seed, rich with promise and possibility, they'd have had to squander enormous amounts of time and energy trying to get a new garden started from nothing.

You get what I'm driving at, I trust.

Wise gardeners don't eat their seed corn.

And wise investors don't spend their principal.

Because in order to grow a fortune, all your efforts should be directed toward making your principal—your nest egg, your nut, your sackful of seeds—grow to the point where it has reached sufficient size that it sustains you all by itself.

It's dumb to be in the business of trying to make a quick bundle in the market, then squandering it all. Instead, you should treat your portfolio like a garden, which is an enterprise involving the mastery of time. It's a vocation that spans many seasons.

Eventually, if you're lucky, wise, and patient, the garden will turn into a magical cornucopia of plenty, no longer even needing hoeing, feeding you grapes and cherries and figs as you recline in your hammock like a sultan.

Raiding the principal in your investment portfolio is even more shortsighted and foolish than it seems, because what you are actually squandering is the incredible wealth-building power of time itself, in the form of compound interest. And, compound interest is truly a many-splendored thing—money without working, tomatoes without weeding or watering.

"Compounding can be magic, even when the compounding is modest," writes veteran value-oriented money manager James Gipson, who runs the highly successful Clipper Fund out of an office in Beverly Hills. "Investors who compound their money in real terms at 7 percent per year will double it in ten years; in forty years they will have *sixteen times* the original amount."

You can't do that by eating your seed corn at the end of each season. Instead, you've got to keep tucking it away, keeping in mind the other seasons to come, so that over time your garden grows into something that sustains you without effort.

Here's another, perhaps slightly extreme example of that magical power. It's often said that when the Indians sold Manhattan Island in 1626 for $24 in beads and trinkets they got ripped off by the white guys. But who knows? Maybe those Indians weren't so dumb. If they'd invested that twenty-four bucks wisely, and it had compounded at 6 percent after taxes for the past 350 years, today it would be worth over $50 *billion.*

Some tomato patch, huh? Another way of looking at the matter is this: for most people, the biggest income stream comes from the wages they make from working. Which is fine, except that there are only so many hours in a day, and only so many work weeks in a lifetime. Even if you're very highly paid, your potential for wealth building is limited by the amount of hours you can work in a day.

For instance, a doctor or a lawyer making $200,000 a year could expect to earn around $8 million in a lifetime—most of which is likely to be gone by retirement age. By contrast, a businessman could retire with $20 million without having to work himself to a frazzle. How? By unhitching his income from his own time. His employees and his capital are "leveraging" his time, multiplying his work, and thus magically expanding the number of hours in his day.

Sure, you probably don't own your own company. But, you can begin to unhitch your income from your own time by building up an investment portfolio that gradually, over time, begins to feed you all by itself.

Investor-author Robert Kiyosaki makes a similar point in his recent bestseller *Rich Dad, Poor Dad*. He tells the story of having been raised by two "dads," one his natural father, a refined scholar who "didn't care about money," and therefore never made much; and a father figure who earned most of his education in the

school of hard knocks but also amassed a fortune. As a boy, Kiyosaki went to the "rich dad" to learn how rich people think about money. Lesson No. 1, the rich dad taught him, is that "the poor and the middle class work for money. The rich have money work for them."

This is easy enough to say, of course—especially if you've already built a portfolio that's working for you. But, the only way to get there is to keep tucking away seeds.

One of the central mysteries of the seed, in fact, is that it is a tiny capsule containing time itself. That is, it's a miniscule packet of DNA-encoded instructions, a food source, and the fantastic *potential* for growth— time in the rough, time unexpressed, time as latent opportunity. It's an "implied" oak tree tucked inside an acorn.

In the same way, your $100,000 portfolio is a $1,000,000 portfolio in the rough.

But, only if you don't eat your seeds.

SINCE THEY ARE BOTH
ESSENTIALLY UNKNOWABLE,
THE PROPER ATTITUDE TOWARD THE
NATURAL WORLD, AND THE STOCK
MARKET, IS ONE OF HUMBLE AWE.

─────

*"Come to the orchard in spring. There is light and wine and
sweethearts in the pomegranate flowers. If you do not come,
these do not matter. If you do come, these do not matter."*
—Sufi poet Jalaluddin Rumi

One of the great delights of the garden is spending so much time in the presence of something so mysterious.

After all, you don't know what drives the shiver through the seed. You don't know why it rains, or does not rain. You don't know what bursts the bud. You don't know where flowers come from. Nobody does.

By the same token, one of the great intellectual delights of investing is to be a small player in international financial markets that are (almost) as vast and mysterious as nature itself. You don't know what's going to happen in the market tomorrow. You don't know which way inflation is headed. There are things about to happen in the world that will directly affect your portfolio that you can't possibly foresee. Nobody can.

That's what makes investing, and gardening, so endlessly interesting.

Even though the financial markets are the aggregate of the behavior of millions of individual humans, their performance—particularly their short-term perform-ance—is so unpredictable that for all practical purposes you might as well consider them unknowable. People talk about "the foreseeable future," but the future is not foreseeable, and anybody who thinks so is a fool. Sure, Ph.D.s have been awarded, and billions of words have been written, in the pursuit of some reliable way to pre-dict the market. But, there is always a ghost in the machine, an unforeseen twist in the road that ultimately turns such efforts into a harsh lesson in humility.

The period of time we're living through right now—filled with rapid technological change, great risk, and great opportunity—has made the markets, and the world, even more unknowable than ever. In 1995, Bill Gates published a book called *The Road Ahead*. People eagerly snapped up the book, hoping to get some clue about what is coming at us in the onrushing future from somebody who presumably might know. Eighteen months after the book was pub-lished Gates rewrote it, having failed to fully grasp the central importance of the Internet in regards to the future. Believe me, if the richest guy in the world (and presumably, one of the smartest) can't see eighteen months ahead, chances are that you can't either.

Another humbling example: the great gray cabal of economists known in the papers as "the experts" have not predicted *a single one* of the nine recessions we've had since World War Two, according to *The Washington Post*. Not the Council of Economic Advisors, not the fifty forecasters known as the Blue Chip Consensus, not the super-smart forecasting staffs of the Federal Reserve Board, or the Congressional Budget Office. Reams of data, stacks of studies, but not much of a gift for prophecy.

So, how should a wise person respond to the mysteries of the market, and the garden? With an exceedingly modest estimate of one's own intelligence, understanding, and abilities. With an absence of pride or foolish bravado. With plenty of patience. In short, with a sense of humble, almost prayerful awe at everything around you that you can neither quite understand nor control.

As a practical matter, lowering your opinion of yourself—and your expectation of success—helps you keep calm when the market drops. It also keeps you calm when the market soars, because as one Wall Street wag remarked, you should "never confuse brilliance with a bull market."

It's an attitude akin to the attitude ancient peoples had toward the natural world. They had reverence for the beauty and intricacy and balance inherent in all natural systems, and their humble place in it all.

Many investors have been ruined when they thought they knew more than they really knew about the market. And, the natural world has been grievously harmed by people who thought they knew more than they really knew about the ways of nature, who lacked awe and reverence for its mysteries.

This is a lesson that gardeners and investors seem to be forever learning over again.

Consider, for instance, all the human attempts to introduce a non-native plant or animal in order to "solve" a problem. In the late nineteenth century, a fast-growing vine called kudzu, native to Japan, was introduced in the American South as a way of combating erosion. Instead, kudzu has become a menace from Louisiana to West Virginia, spreading so rapidly that it chokes out native plants and costs towns and cities millions each year to whack back.

Because somebody way back when thought they knew more than they actually did know, and because they did not have enough humble respect for the mysteries of natural systems, we have a total fiasco on our hands.

In the financial world, no recent story illustrates the perils of this kind of foolish pride as much as the story of the high-flying hedge fund called Long-Term Capital Management. The fund was created in 1994 by famous Wall Street bond trader John W. Meriwether, who told his fat-cat investors (minimum investment: $10 million) that he was creating something the financial world had never seen before. He'd put together a glittering group of geniuses from Wall Street and academia, including two men who had shared a Nobel prize in economics for their work on the pricing of options and other complex financial instruments.

Using complicated computer models, Meriwether and his partners believed they had devised a practically foolproof strategy to detect temporary price distortions between two kinds of bonds. They knew that eventually the prices would equalize, but in the meantime they could use vast sums of borrowed money to exploit these tiny price differences and thus make a profit.

In short, they were using their considerable brainpower to understand and control the most unknowable force in the market, and in life: risk. They had applied arcane equations borrowed from the world of physics to predict these price changes along a bell curve, and they actually thought they had come to understand it.

But only a fool, or someone completely blinded by hubris (or perhaps a Nobel Prize), would ever come to believe that there is any such thing as a completely risk-free investment strategy. No self-respecting gardener would ever believe that, given the vagaries of frost, drought, and pests.

Roger Lowenstein, who wrote a book about the LTCM debacle called *When Genius Failed,* aptly quotes G.K. Chesterton in the book. Life, Chesterton observed, is "a trap for logicians" because it is very nearly, but not quite, reasonable. "It looks just a little more mathematical and regular than it is. Its exactitude is obvious, but its inexactitude is hidden; its wildness lies in wait." Or, as Lowenstein observes, the men who created LTCM "had programmed the market for a cold predictability that it never had."

Even so, for a few years their strategy worked brilliantly. The fund earned more than 40 percent a year during 1995 and 1996, seemingly without risk and with eerie predictability. So certain were the fund's founders of their own invincibility that they had leveraged their bets to an astounding degree. The fund had less than $2.5 billion in assets, but they'd used it as collateral to buy $125 billion in securities. In turn, they used those securities as collateral to engage in complicated transactions affecting $1.25 *trillion* in securities. They were leveraged to the tune of one hundred to one, something almost unheard of in the annals of investment.

Their arrogance knew no bounds.

Meanwhile, the whole house of cards depended on the world behaving as their computer models so confidently promised it would.

Then, rather suddenly, the world did what it always does eventually: it did something unpredictable. The ghost in the machine emerged. The wildness came out of hiding. In August 1998, the Russian government defaulted on its loans, setting in motion a chain reaction of terror. All over the world investors panicked in ways the professors had not predicted.

Their house of cards began to collapse. They began losing $100 million a day—once, an incredible $553 million in one day. Eventually, a group of fourteen private banks pooled resources and bailed the LTCM out. But, not before Meriwether and his partners lost personal fortunes of $1.9 billion.

More than likely, neither you nor I are smart enough to even understand what these big brains were actually trying to do. But, then again, neither were they.

So, rather than starting with the presumption that you are a genuine financial smarty-pants, like the "geniuses" at LTCM, you're better off starting with this assumption: every time I make a decision, there's a good chance—a really good chance—that I'll make a bad one. There is some quirk at the core of being human that leads us to make the wrong decision more often than we make the right one, whether or not we're willing to admit this to ourselves. Therefore, I should limit the number of decisions I make.

Part of the built-in problem with trying to "time" the market (buy low, sell high) is that you have to be right twice—when you buy and when you sell. That simply doubles your chance of being wrong. Most people are lucky to be right, or even half-right, once, let alone twice. Almost nobody is right three times in a row. Warren Buffet's famous dictum that a person should make perhaps twenty major investing decisions in a lifetime is sage advice from someone who has no shortage of brains of his own. But, judging from his own record, it's clear that even he has made his fair share of mistakes. (For instance, his purchase of USAir Group in 1989 was a mistake. This buy, he said later, "displayed exquisite timing. I plunged into the business at almost the exact moment when it ran into problems.")

Therefore, keep the number of decisions you make to a minimum. Good stocks are sometimes called "one decision" stocks for the simple reason that the only real decision you have to make is to buy them in the first place. Then you just hold them more-or-less forever.

It's a way of "leveraging" your limited brains, protecting yourself from stupid mistakes, and simply getting out of the way while your portfolio grows all by itself.

By contrast, approaching the market with an attitude of pompous self-confidence is a good way to learn humility the hard way (and pay for it very dearly). Just ask Terence Odean, a finance professor at the University of California at Davis, who has actually documented the role of arrogance in the returns of investors. In one research paper, he explored the question of why heavy-duty traders, who poured enormous amounts of time and energy into churning their accounts, almost always wound up with mediocre returns. One big reason, he concluded, was "the well-documented tendency for human beings to be overconfident." Despite all the evidence that it is not possible to do it consistently, many of these investors still believed they could "time" the market by buying at the bottom and selling at the top. They jumped out of one stock and into another, convinced that their superior understanding of macroeconomic forces, or some bit of inside information, would give Stock B the edge over Stock A.

Humble awe? Forget it, pal.

The higher the market climbed, the more their portfolios grew, and the more full of themselves these investors became, Dr. Odean found. They were filled with what he describes as a "self-serving attribution bias"—in other words, they tended to take personal credit for all their gains. They thought it was their own breathtaking skill and sheer, unadulterated genius that was fattening their accounts. But when the market tanked, well, that they attributed to "bad luck" or somebody else's foolishness.

It's a kind of neat, closed loop of self-delusion. It's also a way of not learning anything.

With a colleague, Brad M. Barber, Dr. Odean also published a research paper that took another hard look at online traders. Barber and Odean pored over the accounts of 1,607 Internet investors between 1991 and

1997, both before and after they started trading online. It turned out to be a neat little morality play on the perils of overconfidence.

These investors were pretty fair stock-pickers before they plunged into the hyper-accelerated world of online trading. They comfortably outperformed the overall market by roughly 2.4 percent annually, which is not too shabby at all (in fact, better than most professional money managers are). But, that's where they got carried away. Convinced that they were smarter than they actually were, flush with overconfidence from their earlier, off-line success, they started madly trading in cyberspace. Net result: their portfolios, on average, began *under*performing the market by about 3.5 percent a year. The difference between 2.4 over the market and 3.5 percent under it may not seem like much— but over time, those differences can make an enormous difference to your portfolio.

Barber and Odean also noted one other thing about the behavior of these cyber-investors that is perhaps a uniquely twenty-first-century twist on a very old story. Once online, they found, these investors had instant access to "vast quantities of data, often the same data as is available to the professionals." As a consequence, they developed the "illusion of knowledge." Combining the illusion of knowledge with a puffed-up ego is a very bad combination indeed. Yet in the Internet age, we're continuously bombarded by TV ads touting the ease and speed with which people can turn all this instant information into instant wealth. In one famous ad, a tow truck driver buys an island with all his instant information and Internet-enabled trading.

There's just one problem: all that information doesn't necessarily add up to wisdom. It just adds up to... information. In fact, nowadays *too much* information is likely to be as great a problem for investors as too little. Because when you're inundated with data, often at Internet speed, it's easy to become convinced that you actually know something. You develop "the illusion of knowledge," which is just a twenty-first-century version of the ancient sin of hubris, or foolish pride.

Online traders tend to be scornful of stockbrokers—and there are plenty of disreputable or just plain mediocre brokers out there. But frankly, keeping in mind that I am a bear of very little brain, I've always worked with a stockbroker and thought it was worth the fee. It's certainly not wise or necessary to act on every one of their suggestions. But a broker that you respect and trust can provide you with genuinely valuable guidance.

By the same token, nurseryman Andre Viette likes to say that the most important thing you buy at a nursery is information. "When people ask me how to choose a good nursery, my answer is that they should go to the place where they get the best information," he says. "What you're spending on a plant is often insignificant compared to the knowledge you're getting."

A good nursery, or the county extension office, will be happy to provide you with help on what sort of soil preparation you'll need, how much fertilizer to use, and the hardiness of various plants in your gardening zone.

Continue to learn from people who know more than you do. Be humble. Don't get too full of yourself. It's a good way to grow cucumbers, grow a fortune, or live a life.

*K*NOW THY GARDEN,
KNOW THYSELF.

"Though an old man, I am but a young gardener."
—Thomas Jefferson

W hen you see an old gardener out hoeing in his perennial patch, the casual observer would notice nothing more than a humble, stooped-over figure, "a tattered coat upon a stick," calmly cultivating the soil. What the casual observer would probably fail to notice is a person gradually growing wiser, a person becoming a kind of shaman's apprentice to the earth and its ways; a person learning the mastery of their garden, the mastery of time, the mastery of the moment, the mastery of themselves. (Also, perhaps, mastery of that crowd of gremlins peeping out from beneath the rutabaga leaves!)

The proof of all this mastery, of course, is plain to see. Get a load of those vegetables! The lustrous tomatoes smooth as breasts, eggplants the size of barbells with silky, blue-black skin, the corn with perfect kernels ranged down the cob like an embroidery of pearls. But, those are just the outward fruits (and vegetables) of gardening.

The real crop—the real garden—is within. Its harvest is patience. Calm. Self-discipline. What the Taoists call "effortless action."

In the same way, the outward reward of being a successful investor is, well, money. But, the real reward is to be found in the inward garden. It's wisdom. Self-mastery. Courage. Composure.

Average, middling, and flat-out lousy investors tend to approach the stock market as a form of entertainment, or as a way to prove something, or—worst of all—as a sort of analyst's couch where they can work out their personal peculiarities. As financial journalist "Adam Smith" has written, "If you don't know who you are, the stock market is an expensive place to find out!"

By contrast, investors who treat their portfolios like a garden have achieved a Zen-like sense of inner calm and peace and detachment. They've learned to live within the nature of the market and within the nature of themselves, not to try to change it, just peacefully coexist with it.

They've learned the calmness that comes from thinking long, long-term.

They've learned to spend a long time working the soil, slipping a viable seed into the dark, and then waiting.

They've mastered their own emotions, learned to weather out the storms and droughts and frosts and pests, waiting patiently for the crop to ripen.

They've picked an investing strategy that suits their whole life and temperament, their "psychological gardening zone," and calmly stuck with it through thick and thin.

They've put a chair in their garden and just sat there, watching things grow.

They've learned not to worry about other people getting rich faster than they are.

They ignore the frantic scramble to get in on each quarter's hottest fund, ignore "tips," and though they read voraciously, they ignore most of it.

They pay attention to the climate, not the weather.

They consider the eternal, rather than the ephemeral.

They've learned not to eat their seed corn.

They've learned to think not about this season's handful of raspberries, but about the buckets they'll grow a few seasons from now.

They've learned an attitude of humble awe toward the plants, the sun, the moon, the stars, and the stock market.

They're wise enough to know what they don't know.

In short, they grow their portfolio as they grow their garden. Season after season, it grows lush and beautiful, sending out shoots and roots and vines and limbs, flowering and bearing fruit again and again—a magical cornucopia of plenty.

Every summer, if they're lucky, wise and patient, they may even have some tomatoes to give away.

$\mathcal{A}$BOUT THE AUTHOR

Stefan Bechtel has been a successful investor, and a devoted gardener, for more than fifteen years. During the most recent seven-year period—December 31, 1994, to December 31, 2001, which included the NASDAQ's worst year on record—his stock portfolio returned 35.4 percent a year, for a total cumulative gain of 734.6 percent. His favorite flowers are clematis, bearded iris, and lilies of almost any kind. He is the author or coauthor of five previous books, including *The Good Luck Book; Katherine, It's Time; What Women Want;* and *The Practical Encyclopedia of Sex and Health,* which has over one million copies in print and has been translated into Chinese, Korean, and Polish. He is a founding editor of *Men's Health* magazine and president of the Dreaming Hand Foundation.